PENGUIN
SPECIALS

Penguin Specials fill a gap. Written by some of today's most exciting and insightful writers, they are short enough to be read in a single sitting – when you're stuck on a train; in your lunch hour; between dinner and bedtime. Specials can provide a thought-provoking opinion, a primer to bring you up to date, or a striking piece of fiction. They are concise, original and affordable.

To browse digital and print Penguin Specials titles, please refer to **www.penguin.com.au/penguinspecials**

ALSO BY ANNE WITCHARD

Lao She in London

*Thomas Burke's Dark Chinoiserie: Limehouse
Nights and the Queer Spell of Chinatown*

*London Gothic: Place, Space and the Gothic
Imagination*

British Modernism and Chinoiserie

England's Yellow Peril

Sinophobia and the Great War

ANNE WITCHARD

PENGUIN BOOKS

Published by the Penguin Group
Penguin Group (Australia)
707 Collins Street, Melbourne, Victoria 3008, Australia
(a division of Penguin Australia Pty Ltd)
Penguin Group (USA) Inc.
375 Hudson Street, New York, New York 10014, USA
Penguin Group (Canada)
90 Eglinton Avenue East, Suite 700, Toronto, Canada ON M4P 2Y3
(a division of Penguin Canada Books Inc.)
Penguin Books Ltd
80 Strand, London WC2R 0RL, England
Penguin Ireland
25 St Stephen's Green, Dublin 2, Ireland
(a division of Penguin Books Ltd)
Penguin Books India Pvt Ltd
11 Community Centre, Panchsheel Park, New Delhi – 110 017, India
Penguin Group (NZ)
67 Apollo Drive, Rosedale, North Shore 0632, New Zealand
(a division of Penguin New Zealand Pty Ltd)
Penguin Books (South Africa) (Pty) Ltd
Rosebank Office Park, Block D, 181 Jan Smuts Avenue, Parktown North,
Johannesburg 2196, South Africa
Penguin (Beijing) Ltd
7F, Tower B, Jiaming Center, 27 East Third Ring Road North, Chaoyang
District, Beijing 100020, China

Penguin Books Ltd, Registered Offices: 80 Strand, London, WC2R 0RL,
England

First published by Penguin Group (Australia) in association with Penguin
(Beijing) Ltd, 2014

penguin.com.cn

ISBN: 9780143800378

CONTENTS

Preface...1

Inventing Limehouse 8

Perilous Yellowness...24

Sinophilia 42

Chu Chin Chow: 'More Navel than Millinery'.............57

Aftermath: White Girls on Dope...............................72

Broken Blossoms..85

Acknowledgments..89

Notes..90

Preface

Following the outbreak of war in 1914, reports from the battlegrounds shared newspaper inches with accounts of unseemly behaviour in London's dockside district of Limehouse. Here was London's Chinatown, towards which press attention would escalate out of all proportion to its actual significance. This book tells the story of how the tiny Chinese community in London's East End became a principal scapegoat for England's wartime vulnerabilities at home.

The East End-West End division of the empire's capital had, since its late-nineteenth-century expansion, become a microcosm of imperial anxiety. In 1914, just as in the Boer War of 1899, worrying numbers of working-class men from London's poorer districts, particularly the East End, were found to be physically unfit for recruitment, reviving Darwinian concerns about racial degeneration of the British people. In 1911, the National Council of Public Morals had been driven by the new pseudo-science of eugenics to declare 'race-regeneration' a national imperative, appealing to women to head the vanguard of a battle for sexual purity. With the onset of the war, the campaign was given renewed impetus.

Of particular focus was the disreputable behaviour of certain white women among the Chinese in Limehouse. It was reasoned that racial mixing with non-whites undermined the hierarchical structure of race that upheld the imperial rationale and could not be tolerated. Dramatic headlines focused on the problem of interracial alliances between 'yellow' men and white women. This was accounted for not as conceivably as it might have been by the almost total dearth of Chinese women in maritime Limehouse, but by the susceptibility of a certain type of white woman to 'Oriental depravity'. Silly girls, devoid of moral sense, were identified as the target of an East End Yellow Peril.

Chinese customs that hitherto had been accepted now caused alarm. Gambling had been more or less ignored until it became a wartime issue. The fear was that working-class wives were squandering their separation allowances playing *fantan* and *puck-a-pu,* or worse still consorting with Chinese who smoked opium. While opium smoking had frequently brought members of the Chinese population into conflict with the police, new regulations imposed by successive wartime clauses of the Defence of the Realm Act (DORA, as it was popularly known) outlawed the drug, thereby criminalising a major portion of the community. Forgotten was the ignominious history of British involvement in the global opium trade as a moral battle was waged on the home front against Chinese vice. Doping came to be seen not just as a deviant activity but something thoroughly unpatriotic. DORA worked effectively to alienate 'the Chinaman' and his subhuman enslavement to opium.

The reading public had been aware of Limehouse as London's Chinatown for some decades. Operations between British trading companies and the Far East were established in the 1860s, since which time merchant steamship companies had been employing cheap labour signed on in China's treaty ports. London's already cosmopolitan East End became more so with an influx of Chinese, lascars and Malays. Along the dockside streets of Limehouse Causeway and Pennyfields, a few settled Chinese catered to their sojourning compatriots, running grocery stores, association halls, restaurants, laundries, lodging houses and places for opium smoking and gambling. The journalist George R. Sims was the first to use the term 'China Town' with regard to the district in 1905:

The bus terminus – the West India Dock Station – is an excellent point from which to take a trip around Limehouse. Close at hand is the Causeway, the Chinese quarter . . . in Limehouse the Asiatic seafaring man is still a conspicuous note. You will find specimens of him – Oriental, mysterious, romantic – at almost every turn. At the corner of the Causeway, as we turn into it in search of 'China Town in London', we come upon a group of Lascars in their picturesque little round caps chatting together . . . let us make our way through narrow, winding China Town. There is no mistake about the Chinese element. The Chinese names are up over the doors of the little shops, and as we peer inside them we see the unmistakable Celestial behind the counter and Chinese inscriptions on the walls. At the back of one little shop is an opium den. If we enter we shall find only a couple of clients, for this is not the hour.[1]

The Limehouse of legend encompassed Ratcliffe Highway, Limehouse Causeway, Pennyfields and Narrow Street, the East and West India Dock Roads, Amoy Place, and Pekin, Canton and Nankin Streets. In the years before 1914, it was generally accepted as an inevitable consequence of empire that the humbler citizens of England's trading concessions and the lesser employees of its steamship lines might journey to this outpost of its mighty capital. In wartime, though, the very existence of foreign quarters threatened the idea of a nation wishing to believe itself socially and ethnically homogenous. Newspapers targeted foreigners living in

Britain as the enemy within. The Chinese population, linked to drug trafficking, white slavery (the abduction and trafficking of women for prostitution) and subversion generally, was declared a moral menace.

At the same time, the war brought more Chinese into Limehouse as men filled the berths in merchant ships left empty by conscripted sailors, infuriating the National Union of Seamen and provoking angry questions in Parliament. In 1915 it was reported that some 14224 Chinese were employed aboard British ships. Naturally, the influx had its effect on Chinatown.[2] 'The invasion is becoming serious', pronounced *The Times*, employing wartime rhetoric in a foreboding pronouncement warning of the spread of Chinese beyond the traditional confines of Limehouse.[3]

As the war dragged on and labour shortages pressed, local employers would begin to recruit Chinese into work beyond that of shipping and docks jobs. In 1917, the Bethnal Green Board of Guardians thought to give jobs in its workhouse to some Chinese who had been 'submarined whilst in boats carrying provisions to England'.[4] The decision caused a row but nonetheless was implemented. Less successful was the overburdened London Hospital's attempt to employ 'Chinese gentlemen' as kitchen orderlies and porters. The other staff refused to work with them so the proposal had to be abandoned.[5]

Towards the end of the war, Chinese labour would be used on aerodrome construction for the new Air Ministry, but by this time boycotting Chinese workmen had become diplomatically difficult. In August 1917, China had become an ally, declaring war on Austria-Hungary and Germany, and providing manpower in the form of the hundred-thousand-strong Chinese Labour Corps, Chinese labourers who had been shipped out to serve on the Western Front as manual labour. Yet such was the level of hostility directed towards the Chinese that their contributions on behalf of Britain's war effort did nothing to change public opinion. When the Armistice was declared in 1918, the Chinese Labour Corps continued to be employed, engaged in hazardous work such as mine clearance, filling in trenches and burying bodies. Despite their efforts, none were permitted to enter Great Britain. Furthermore, thanks to a 1919 extension of the Aliens Restriction Act, Chinese seamen who had served in the Merchant Navy were not given permission to remain in England.

While the trade unions and the newspapers had played their part, nowhere were popular cultural representations of the Chinese more effectively parlayed than in the fictions of two writers who, unwitting or otherwise, ensured that the terrors of a fearsome Yellow Peril and the dark doings of Limehouse would be a media staple of the decades to come. Between Thomas Burke's tales of Limehouse love and Sax Rohmer's Yellow Peril thrillers, the Victorian narrative tradition of dockside Limehouse as a place where gentlemen went sometimes to smoke opium developed into a lurid wartime literature of 'Chinamen', flappers, sex and dope.

Inventing Limehouse

'A little world I created for my own purpose and called Limehouse, as Rider Haggard created a world for his purposes and called it Africa'[6]

– Thomas Burke, *City of Encounters: A London Divertissement*, 1932

It is a curious irony that an increasingly hostile perception of the Chinese in Britain coincided with a period of utmost national vulnerability for China. The years from the widely reported Boxer Uprising of 1900 until the establishment of the Nationalist Government in the late 1920s saw a proliferation of pernicious Chinese stereotypes across Western media. An amalgamation of Yellow Peril fears – the Victorian wariness of East End opium dens, newspaper stories of Boxer atrocities, the purported infamies of the decadent scions of an ailing Qing Dynasty and other fabulous reports from China correspondents – were fanned into a rabid Sinophobia that found its chief outlet in the wartime discovery of London's Chinatown. Two newspapermen, Thomas Burke and Arthur Sarsfield

8

Ward (better known by his pseudonym of Sax Rohmer) would be credited with inventing the myth that was Chinese Limehouse. Rohmer would resurrect late-Victorian invasion fiction with his creation of that Yellow Peril fiend incarnate, Dr Fu Manchu, while Burke would stir prurient imaginings with his tales of illicit Limehouse love.

In the unsuspecting summer months of 1914, Thomas Burke, occasional journalist and literary aspirant, was ideally positioned to peddle his own manuscript around town. During his seven years as secretary to London's leading literary agent, C. F. Cazenove, Burke had developed a wide circle of literary connections. Some of his poetry espousing a radical socialist stance had appeared in Ford Madox Ford's advanced literary journal, *The English Review*, and coupled with Cazenove's endorsement, young Burke became someone to watch. His collection of slumland stories titled *Limehouse Nights: Tales of Chinatown* met with favourable interest, but the gathering events of that summer would mean that two more years would pass before his book was taken on.

By the time *Limehouse Nights* was finally published in 1916, it had already been turned down by no less than twelve publishers. The fact of relations between Chinese men and white women had become an issue of critical national concern, and no publisher wanted to risk such incendiary subject matter. The frowsy dockside opium dens and illegal gambling parlours, haunts of Burke's displaced Chinamen and the ringletted Cockney waifs of their affections, were deemed too subversive.

In his rejection letter to Burke, prominent publisher William Heinemann blamed the current 'constrained condition of mind', indicated recently, as he pointed out, by the suppression of D. H. Lawrence's *The Rainbow*, which the Commissioner of Police had pronounced to be 'a mass of obscenity of thought, ideas and action throughout'.[7] Published in 1915, Lawrence's provocative novel was prosecuted under the Obscene Publications Act for being likely to affect national moral well-being, and his publishers were forced to withdraw the book. While a lesbian encounter in the chapter 'Shame' was what ultimately condemned *The Rainbow*, Heinemann considered the prosecution 'a good illustration of the tendencies just now, and an indication that the interest in the psychology of the pervert is not likely to appeal as long as the war lasts.'[8]

The case against *The Rainbow* focused public anxieties about 'Germanic' degeneracy in British culture, and it would take a brave publisher to take on *Limehouse Nights* with its frank and uncritical depiction of Chinatown life in all its perverse irregularity. Here were tales of abused little girls like Lucy Burrows, rescued from an opium den by her poet lover, Cheng Huan, or Pansy Greers, who takes deadly revenge on the rapist

Tai Fu; of Cantonese-speaking copper's nark Poppy Sturdish and duped Sway Lim, who gets his revenge; of Jewell Angel, the acrialist, fatally sabotaged for snubbing 'half-caste' Cheng Brander; of suicide victims Beryl Hermione Chudder and Wing Foo, her pimp. There are the sordid psychodramas of Daffodil Flanagan and her lover, Fung Tsin, and of treacherous Gracie Goodnight, who murders her nasty boss, Kang Foo Ah, and gets away with it. On a happier note, but astonishing for its day, pretty teenaged prostitute Marigold Vassiloff and good-natured Tai Ling, one of three contenders for the paternity of her child, live happily ever after.

Heinemann was not the only publisher to voice concerns over Burke's choice of subject matter. Andrew Melrose, a well-known publisher of theological works, despite having published some controversial fiction himself, responded unequivocally that he wanted 'nothing to do with books about white girls and chinks'.[9] For Stanley Unwin, 'Church of England business' comprised a substantial part of his turnover, and Burke's tales of lowlife love in London's Limehouse docks 'represented too startling a departure from the character of our publications'. As he recalled some years later:

It is astonishing in life how frequently the most attractive proposals come one's way at the moment when it is impracticable to accept them. It must be remembered that the attitude towards books was much more squeam-ish and puritanical in 1914 than it has been since 1918.[10]

Yet so impressed was Unwin with Burke's evocative rendering of London life that he commissioned a different book from him, *Nights in Town: A London Autobiography*, and would subsequently offer him a job upon Cazenove's death in 1915.

Thomas Burke was deemed unfit for military service and wound up spending his war years working for the American branch of the Department of Information. Physically, he was unprepossessing, bespectacled and very small in stature. The Welsh author Caradoc Evans, to whom Burke would dedicate *Limehouse Nights*, was editing for Hulton Publications in Fleet Street when he first met Burke, who had come in looking for a job. Evans describes his first impression of the author:

Thomas Burke in 1917, at the age of 31

I raised my eyes and saw a narrow, slight strip of a figure. I saw a black-and-white line: black clothes, white face, and thick black hair shining as if it had been pasted down on a dummy head. The hair was the only considerable thing about my visitor; the body was tiny, so were the head, the nose, the hands, and the feet. He looked at me through spectacles, the metal sides of which had been repaired with black yarn . . . He neither deplored nor bragged his poverty . . . Within a month of this he obtained fame with his *Nights in Town*, and within a year with his *Limehouse Nights*.[11]

As 1915 drew to its grim close, Burke was still typing in the office of Allen and Unwin and trying, unsuccessfully, to place his Chinese stories. London's publishing industry had suffered severe setbacks, and publishers, short both of paper and print facilities, were cutting their lists and postponing publications rather than taking on new authors. It was then that a harried Grant Richards, whose discoveries included George Bernard Shaw, G. K. Chesterton and James Joyce, finally got around to reading Burke's manuscript. With his usual prescience, Richards made up his mind straight away that despite anticipating trouble from the book, 'Thomas Burke and *Limehouse Nights* were just too good to let go'.[12] Aware of the doubtful nature of what was deemed acceptable to the authorities, Grant Richards took the precaution of soliciting letters of support from eminent literary figures, among them George Bernard Shaw, Arnold Bennett and Ford Madox Ford, who dutifully took the typescript of *Limehouse Nights* back to the trenches with him, reading it to the sound of Boche shells. As for the immorality, Ford commented: 'I never thought about it, so that it cannot be so very immoral'.[13]

While Ford's nonchalance was encouraging, *Limehouse Nights: Tales of Chinatown* was published in 1916 to predictable notoriety. The book was banned by the national circulating libraries, Boots and W. H. Smith. Burke was condemned in strong terms as a 'blatant agitator' in the *Times Literary Supplement* for his evocative portrayal of a multiracial East End: 'In place of the steady, equalised light which he should have thrown on that pestiferous spot off the West India Dock Road', blasted the review, 'he has been content . . . with flashes of limelight and fireworks'.[14] Grant Richards was tipped off by Bennett – in his new capacity as Director of Propaganda for France at the Ministry of Information – that the possibility of securing a conviction was being 'most seriously discussed at headquarters and that he himself feared the worst'.[15]

By 1916, England was in the thick of war and would suffer heavy casualties in the Battle of the Somme. Developing in tandem with the events at the battlefront was the prevailing mood of cultural solidarity at home.

The moral health of Londoners was now considered interdependent with racial fitness, and general English well-being was seen as crucial to the country's defence capabilities. The publication of *Limehouse Nights* coincided with a series of stirring addresses by Arthur Winnington-Ingram, Bishop of London, in a pamphlet titled *Cleansing London*, a patriotic plea that linked the front line with the home front as a moral battlefield. If the war was to be a true victory, warned Ingram, it was up to the women of London to 'purge the heart of the Empire before the boys come back.'[16] The standard newspaper fare of gambling raids, opium smoking and hatchet fights in Limehouse was joined by accounts of English women whose wayward behaviour was undermining the security of the country. Burke himself got cold feet and demanded that Grant Richards cancel the clause in their contract which would have made him financially responsible for the costs of defending any action brought against *Limehouse Nights*.

Burke had every reason to worry about prosecution. Stories about Tai Fu and Pansy Greers, or Kang Fu Ah and Gracie Goodnight, symbolised all too vividly the degeneration of British society. Eugenicists and social Darwinists had maintained for some years that the nation was in a state of physical and moral decline. H. G. Wells reviewed the book and although he was in praise of its 'romantic force and beauty', his personal response was one of aversion to 'the rather horrible sexual circulation'.[17] Burke's tales of Limehouse love troubled their clearly delineated concepts of purity and pollution that had become insistent undercurrents of early twentieth-century thinking.

In conservative quarters the war was heartily welcomed for its 'purifying fire', as sculptor and Royal Academician W. R. Colton put it. Colton singled out in his harangue 'the likes of Oscar Wilde, Aubrey Beardsley, and others'. The war, it seemed, might finally rid the country of degenerate foreign influence spread by the spiritual descendants of Wilde – 'the futurists, the cubists, the whole school of decadent novelists'.[18]

The eminent Victorian man of letters Edmund Gosse, for whom England had many enemies within, was stronger and shrewder still in his condemnation. Gosse, who was then the librarian of the House of Lords Library, produced an essay in 1914 titled 'War and Literature'. The essay was a diatribe against England's hedonism, moral laxity and lethargic dilettantism, subtly couched in analogy to Chinese decadence. Gosse imagined the war as 'the sovereign disinfectant . . . its red stream of blood is the Condy's Fluid that cleans out the stagnant pools and clotted channels of the intellect'. England had 'awakened from an opium-dream of comfort', he declared – canny rhetoric indeed.[19]

'Conditions for launching a Chinese villain on the market were ideal'

– Sax Rohmer, 'How Fu Manchu was Born',
This Week, 1957

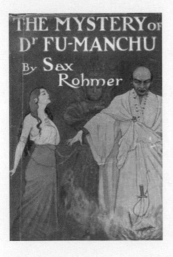

First edition cover of *The Mystery of Dr Fu-Manchu*, 1913

At the same time that Thomas Burke had been trying to place his Limehouse stories, another writer who was doing the rounds of Fleet Street was more astute in his assessment of the prevailing conservatism. Sax Rohmer, born Arthur Sarsfield Ward, was the man behind the phenomenally successful Fu Manchu series, featuring the diabolical Dr Fu Manchu, famously described as 'the yellow peril incarnate in one man'.[20]

Rohmer's debut novel, *The Mystery of Dr Fu-Manchu*, was published in the year before the war began.

The book was a collation of various magazine stories published in the preceding years. Limehouse is not depicted as significant in this early novel, and it was not until the war that Fu Manchu would reside in Chinese Limehouse and endow the area with his mythical and dread-inspiring force.

Rohmer's evil genius Fu Manchu plots a global takeover by a yellow empire from his headquarters in an East End riverside warehouse and has a poison-manufacturing laboratory in an abandoned ship on the Thames. The closest *The Mystery of Dr Fu-Manchu* comes to depicting a dockside Chinatown is Singapore Charlies, a dope shop off the Ratcliffe Highway, an East End street that, in the nineteenth century, was notorious for vice and crime, most notably a series of brutal killings known as the Ratcliffe Highway murders.

The location of Singapore Charlies followed in the Victorian literary tradition of Charles Dickens, Arthur Conan Doyle and Oscar Wilde. Rohmer, and Burke for that matter, were well read in the confluence of documentary and fictional evidence that formed the image of London's East End and its scattering of Chinese residents in the nineteenth century. Burke would describe this literary circulation in a later book, *English Night-Life*:'

In the [Ratcliffe] Highway at that time a number of Chinese had their homes, and many of them kept opium rooms.

One of them known as Johnson's was put into literature by Dickens. He described it in *Edwin Drood* as the house frequented by John Jasper for his secret indulgences.[21]

Ratcliffe Highway ran between the districts of Shadwell and Limehouse, close to the docks, and was known as Tiger Bay on account of its predatory prostitutes. In his book *Low-Life Deeps*, journalist James Greenwood described the late-night merchants of sex as 'flashily bedizened and painted prowlers' who go out to 'beguile and plunder' the sailors 'as systematically as did the foot-pads and highwaymen of olden times'.[22]

After Britain's victories in the Opium Wars (1839–1842 and 1856–1860), portrayal of the Chinese would reflect the new balance of power that followed in the wake of negotiations over treaty ports and indemnities. In order to conceal the contradictions and hypocrisy of British policy, a wave of anti-opium agitation at home was responsible for propagating damaging images of Chinese depravity. Pamphleteers, politicians and the press began to portray the Chinese as heathens and fools in thrall to a corrupt monarch and enslaved by opium. Dickens had commissioned one of the first published portrayals of an East End opium room in 1866. 'Lazarus, Lotus-Eating' was preoccupied with the orientalising effect of opium on the complexion of English women, something that would become a convention of Rohmer's wartime fiction.

Literature could not help but be informed by the political current. Four years after he commissioned 'Lazarus, Lotus-Eating', Dickens would depict the degeneracy of opium use in his own fiction. His portrayal of John Jasper's vicious habit in *The Mystery of Edwin Drood* transformed the noxious but generally harmless sailor's resort described by reporters into the opium den of Victorian Gothic, a perilous place, its occupants invariably iniquitous: 'Said Chinaman convulsively wrestles with one of his many Gods or Devils, perhaps, and snarls horribly. The Lascar laughs and dribbles at the mouth.'[23]

Arthur Conan Doyle paints an equally chilling picture in 'The Man with the Twisted Lip'. One of his most atmospheric scenes is when Watson and Holmes go to an East End opium den. In *The Picture of Dorian Gray*, Oscar Wilde would refer to Greenwood's description of a dance hall on the Ratcliffe Highway for his sinister dockside opium dive. Dorian drags aside a tattered green curtain and enters:

a long, low room which looked as if it had once been a third-rate dancing-saloon. Shrill flaring gas-jets, dulled and distorted in the fly-blown mirrors that faced them, were ranged round the walls. Greasy reflectors of ribbed tin backed them, making quivering discs of light . . . Some Malays were crouching by a little charcoal stove playing with bone counters and showing their white teeth as they chattered. In one corner with his head buried in his arms, a sailor sprawled over a table, and by the tawdrily painted bar that ran across one complete side stood two haggard women mocking an old man.[24]

Directly following the publication of Wilde's novel, the Surgeon Major, addressing the annual meeting of the British Medical Association, proclaimed that the importance of getting rid of the 'opium smoking saloons' in East London could not be overestimated.[25]

At the same time, there were flickerings of cultural sensitivity from liberal quarters. An 1895 article titled 'Chinese London and its Opium Dens' appeared in the popular periodical *The Gentleman's Magazine*. Despite the focus of its title, the article described the dockside Chinatown in terms of a mundane dependence: 'It exists by and for the Chinese firemen, seamen, stewards, cooks, and carpenters who serve on board the steamers plying between China and the port of London'.[26]

After the arrival of the new century, the mainstream press took up the cause, making light-hearted attempts to dispel the gloom of the opium den. Typical of such philanthropic irony was novelist Walter Besant's account:

We have read accounts of the dreadful place have we not? Greatly to my disappointment, because when one goes to an opium den for the first time one expects a creeping of the flesh at least, the place was neither dreadful nor horrible . . . Except for the smell of the place, which was overwhelming, the musical instrument was the only horror of the opium den.[27]

These people were 'colourful and harmless' concluded George A. Wade in 'The Cockney John Chinaman', thoroughly debunking the Chinese of late-Victorian Gothic fiction:

The Chinaman in Limehouse is a most peaceable, inoffensive, harmless character. He is on good terms with his neighbours, most of whom speak well of him. He is picturesque in a region where it is sadly needed; his street is unique in this country.[28]

In 1902, the fact of mixed marriages in 'Oriental London' was introduced and calmly explained in the pages of *Living London*. The offspring resulting from such unions was pronounced charming:

All the established Chinamen have married Englishwomen, and in their case marriage has not been a failure, for they seem happy. Their children look healthy and are comfortably dressed, and most of them are very nice-looking. These dark-haired, black-eyed boys and girls, with the rosy cheeks and happy looks, are real little pictures.[29]

A Limehouse shop front as
published in *Living London*

But with the start of the war, newspaper articles about
'Oriental London' and 'Cockney John Chinaman' would
take on a decidedly different tone. Britain's tabloid-read-
ing classes were assured of a hygienic war that would
sweep away the corrupt and degenerate legacy of Oscar
Wilde and his like and cleanse the nation of decadent
foreign influence. It dawned on Sax Rohmer that the
small community of yellow seamen who lodged in the
riverside streets down by the West India Docks was an
ideal fictive scapegoat for this raft of middle-class moral
concern. The idea of London's moral Yellow Peril took a
firm hold with the progression of the war, helped along
by Rohmer's 1915 novel *The Yellow Claw*, which located
Chinese Limehouse in proper pestiferous detail.

Perilous Yellowness

Sax Rohmer's earliest stories about Fu Manchu had been serialised in the years preceding the war following agitation in the press. Riots had broken out in the East End over cheap Chinese labour and allegations of organised illegal immigration abounded. The menace of 'the yellow workman' inured to the lowest standard of material comfort had been widely reported from the United States and so the British working class was well instructed in the threat to its interests posed by Chinese immigration. We need to remember this in order to understand how – from 1914 to 1918 – the reading public was ready to believe the Yellow Peril a significant threat.

The phenomenon of yellow invasion first began as press speculation in the United States in the 1870s with the influx of Chinese workers into the white-dominated labour market. The strongly patriotic *Leslie's Illustrated Newspaper* began a series in 1870 titled 'The Coming Man' designed to inform the American public about Chinese immigration. The illustrations detailed a never-ending disembarkment of Chinese men on American shores, indistinguishable with their long queues and nonde-script coolie clothing. Their inexorably alien ways as well as the extensive array of employment undertaken for rock-bottom wages were shown to result in the reaction of 'native artisans' to 'rise against the Celestials . . . in riotous opposition'.[30] The discussion was provoked for various ends by politicians and religious fundamentalists as well as labour activists, intensifying prejudice against the Chinese worker: 'He pilfers we are told; he lies, he is dirty, he smokes opium, is full of bestial devices – a pagan, and what is far more important, yellow! All his sins are to be pardoned but the last'.[31]

The stereotypes deployed in 'The Coming Man' would harden over the ensuing decade into a general media barrage depicting the Chinese as vicious and dehumanised, an unevolved, barbarous race that posed a perilous threat to the cultural and moral integrity of white America. A series of laws and acts were put in place to restrict Chinese immigration, culminating in the infamous Chinese Exclusion Act of 1882 which suspended immigration of Chinese labour for a period of ten years. In 1892, despite strong objections from the Chinese government, the United States Congress voted to renew exclusion for another ten years.

Yellowness was inextricably linked to late-nineteenth-century thinking about the Far East. It was during this

An illustrated caricature of a Chinese immigrant in 'The Coming Man'

period that an association between yellow and skin colour became conventional. Laboriously constructed hierarchical racial categorisations of a yellow East 'became fully agreed upon in the West', notes the historian and Sinologist Michael Keevak, when 'it was accepted as a feature of the perilousness of the region'.[32] The perceived attributes of yellowness would pervade well into the new century on both sides of the Atlantic.

The intellectual climate of Darwinism made nations increasingly self-conscious of their 'fitness' in the evolutionary struggle for survival. This was particularly so in Britain, where the imperial optimism and vigour of the first half of the nineteenth century had been succeeded by uneasiness. The new imperialism of the 1890s was driven by insecurity and defensiveness in the face of political and commercial challenge from rival powers.

Concerns about racial deterioration among the lower classes were matched by fears that the ruling classes were riddled with moral decadence. In 1893, historian and educationalist Charles Henry Pearson's *National Life and Character: A Forecast* had startled the Victorians by articulating their worst fears: the future possibility of competition from a modernised, mechanised China. Pearson's book challenged conventional sureties regarding Anglo-Saxon expansion and progress. He argued that it was the 'Black and Yellow' races who were now in the ascendant.[33] Victorian susceptibilities regarding degeneration, coupled with stunning evidence of a rising Japanese military, gave the Yellow Peril a dreadful inevitability.

We might date the start of an obsession with a Yellow Peril in British popular culture from 1898, its most notable marker being the publication that year of M. P. Shiel's novel *The Yellow Danger*, which would be directly influential on Rohmer's Yellow Peril fiction. Shiel had worked up the novel from his weekly serial 'The Empress of the Earth: The Tale of the Yellow War', which was fired off some months earlier in *Short Stories* magazine after 'some trouble broke out in China'.[34]

The trouble referred to was a diplomatic crisis in China that had looked set to topple Britain's dominating influence among the European nations. After China's surprise defeat in the First Sino-Japanese War

in 1895, the Western powers had engaged in an ignominious squabble over treaty concessions and spheres
of influence. Two years later in 1897, the killing of two
missionary priests provided a pretext for Kaiser Wilhelm
to dispatch a couple of warships to the port city of
Kiaochow (now Jiaozhou) on the Shandong Peninsula.
Tsar Nicholas responded by seizing the strategically
important Port Arthur (now Lüshun), an ice-free port in
the north of China on the Yellow Sea. Russia had by now
pushed the Trans-Siberian Railway across Manchuria
and built a branch line to Port Arthur. Then France
occupied Hainan Island in the south. It was not just that
manoeuvres between the continental powers looked set
to oust England's long held predominance in China,
but it was feared that the German action, imitated by
others, might push China into military collusion with
Japan against the West. This was a frightening prospect
indeed, and the heightened public interest led to the
commissioning of 'The Empress of the Earth'.

Shiel's *Short Stories* serial ran weekly in 1898 and
proved wildly popular with the public. Each week he
interwove stories from the previous week's news events
into a fantasy of future global war. England, with no allies
and enfeebled by 'the rapacity and selfish greed of her
competitors' (Russia, Germany and France), lay vulnerable to an approaching 'locust swarm of the yellow races'.[35]
It was underpinned by a combination of contemporary

reportage and flights of wild speculation, much of which were derived from journalist W. T. Stead's reportage of the First Sino-Japanese War during 1894–1895. In 1893, Stead had invited Shiel to collaborate with him on the launch of a popular weekly, *The Daily Paper*, a key feature of which would be a continuing serial called 'The Romance of the World'. The idea was to incorporate leading global events into fictional form in order to attract those readers who would not read politics unless served with the sauce of a good story. We only have to turn to Stead's own articles about the Sino-Japanese conflict in his paper, *Review of Reviews*, to account for the articulation of a pan-Asian Yellow Peril in *The Yellow Danger*. In the second year of the war, news of atrocities committed by Japanese soldiers at Port Arthur had begun to break. Stead explained the Port Arthur massacre in terms of Darwinian notions of racial atavism:

> Until they captured Port Arthur, the Japanese behaved as if they really had been civilized more than skin deep. After the capture of the Chinese stronghold the aboriginal savage broke out, and the mild-mannered well-drilled Japanese soldiers indulged in several days' cold-blooded massacre . . . The Japanese although they use the mitrailleuse and torpedo-boat, are Asiatics who for centuries have carried on war in the regular Asiatic fashion. It is not therefore surprising they should have had a bad relapse.[36]

He speculated that if Japan were to modernise her backward neighbour, then China's huge population might one day be mobilised to create an army capable of turning the Europeans out of the Far East, and even of invading Europe itself:

> It was not by remaining in the ancient ways and by reverently nursing every mouldy fragment of medievalism that time had spared that the Japs were able to grasp the thunderbolts with which they have hurled China from her ancient throne in Manchuria and Korea. The Japs have won because they were progressive with a vengeance, and having once grasped the new ideas, carried them out to their ultimate logical conclusion.[37]

The 'Empress of the Earth' – cut back by a third – was rushed out later that year as *The Yellow Danger*. The narrative thrust revolved around a conspiracy to oust England from her predominance in China. Its jingoism was underscored with the rhetoric of Christianity: England 'having a genuine supremacy of racial value and valour' must 'like the Christ of the nations, with many an agony of sweat and blood, redeem mankind'.[38] Shiel didn't shy away from the horrors Europe might expect at the hands of a conquering Orient: 'The reign of hell which had followed upon some Japanese victories during the Sino-Japanese War was well known

M. P. Shiel's *The Yellow Danger*, first published in 1898

in Europe. If China had fared so at the hand of Japan, how would Europe fare at the hand of China led by Japan . . . ?'[39]

During his lifetime, *The Yellow Danger* was Shiel's most successful book, going through numerous editions, particularly when the Boxer Uprising of 1899–1901 seemed to confirm his fictional portrayal of Chinese hostility towards the West. Obituaries were printed in *The Times* for the leading members of the foreign community who had supposedly perished at the hands of these bloodthirsty barbarians. *The New York Times* relayed how the Boxers had 'hacked and stabbed both dead and wounded, cutting off their heads and carrying these through the streets on their rifles'.[40] The fictional scenario of *The Yellow Danger* was described as imminent in '*The Times*' reporting of a Boxer massacre in Peking, an incident that would later prove to be fictitious. Readers were warned to prepare for 'a universal uprising of the yellow race'.[41] Following this came the first English usage of the term Yellow Peril recorded by the Oxford English Dictionary. It was taken from a *Daily News* report of 21 July 1900, which had described the uprising as a massacre, and the term was explained as 'supposed danger that the Asiatic peoples would overwhelm the white or overrun the world'.

Much has been written about Sax Rohmer's debt to M. P. Shiel regarding the genesis of Dr Fu Manchu, who bears many resemblances to Shiel's evil mastermind, Dr Yen How. What has been overlooked are the chilling resonances of Rohmer's reworking of Shiel's original Yellow Peril scenario of a beleaguered England.

'The Yellow Peril incarnate in one man'

– Sax Rohmer,
The Mystery of Dr Fu-Manchu, 1913

The endlessly and ubiquitously re-quoted description of Dr Fu Manchu as 'the Yellow Peril incarnate in one man' has an agglomeration of precedents. From the time of the massively sensationalised Boxer trouble, the yellow man in the British press would invariably stand for all that was fearsome and abhorrent, and for everything that posed a threat to Britain's imperial and domestic status quo. During the General Election of 1906, negative attention was drawn to the Chinese community in England by the efforts of union leaders and working men's associations. They had been pressing the government to compel shipping companies to engage British-only crews and to strengthen the Aliens Act, which had been introduced in 1905 to control immigration by preventing designated paupers and criminals from entering the country. In the same year, an editorial in the *Manchester Evening Chronicle* had rejoiced 'that the dirty, destitute, diseased, verminous and criminal foreigner who dumps himself on our soil and rates simultaneously, shall be forbidden to land'.[42] This was followed up in a *Daily Mail* report in December 1906, protesting that a continued influx of Chinese into Liverpool was 'driving English men and women into the workhouse' because 'a Chinaman could live on the smell of an oil rag'.[43] James Sexton, General Secretary of the National Union of Dock Labourers and member of the Liverpool City Council, was the most vociferous of anti-Chinese voices: 'He comes here like an international octopus spreading its tentacles everywhere', warned Sexton.[44] Not only was English labour being displaced by Chinese labour, but the debasing of English women meant that 'a new race was springing up'. Sexton raised the spectre of miscegenation that was to become so insistent during the war that the 'next generation of hybrid Englishmen would not be worthy of the land they live in'.[45] Prompted by this tirade, the city council set up a commission of enquiry into the Liverpool Chinese. Although gratuitous and prurient in many details, its findings repudiated the more sensational of Sexton's sexual and criminal allegations.

Because the image of London's Chinese Quarter at the fin de siècle was inextricably linked with the opium den, changing attitudes towards opium would inform the way the district was envisaged during the war years. New legal controls were introduced, alienating the consumption of opiates as concerns arose about soldiers self-medicating with doses of cocaine and heroin. The drugs might be bought on gelatine sheets bound in handsome leather wallets from Harrods or Fortnum & Mason and sent out to soldiers at the front along with tins of salmon and socks. Subsequently they might be obtained from Soho prostitutes, allegedly supplied by the Chinese.

As drug use became criminalised, Chinese Limehouse became synonymous with crime. Rohmer's novel *The Yellow Claw* was published in 1916 following the success of *The Mystery of Dr Fu-Manchu* three years earlier. He introduced a new arch-villain, the shadowy Mr King, boss of a worldwide opium syndicate fronted by a ginger wholesaling company, Kan-Suh Concessions, in Limehouse Causeway: 'A high priest of the cult has arisen, and from a parent lodge in Peking he has extended his offices to kindred lodges in most of the capitals of Europe and of Asia.' Mira Leroux, wife of celebrity author Henry Leroux, is a victim of the opium cult which is decimating the upper echelons of artistic London. On her disappearance, Detective Gaston Max assures the distraught Leroux that it 'is only a question of time . . . and you will have the satisfaction of knowing that – though at a great cost to yourself – this dreadful evil has been stamped out, that this obscene yellow peril has been torn from the heart of society.'[46]

The Yellow Claw was successful because it played to the public's concerns not just about aliens in its midst, but also about the licentious behaviour of the British elite and London's West End demi-monde. The novel was released as a film in 1921, two years before the first Fu Manchu book was filmed. The evil Mr King only ever appears as a pair of claw-like yellow hands, firstly at the neck of a doomed flapper and finally disappearing into the waters of the Thames. Years after the Fu Manchu books had eclipsed *The Yellow Claw* in public consciousness, Rohmer would say that a real-life Mr King had been the inspiration for the character of Fu Manchu. He had been assigned, he claimed, by a Fleet Street newspaper in 1911 to write an article about a mysterious Limehouse crime boss. When a 'tall, dignified Chinese, wearing a fur-collared overcoat' stepped out of the car, Rohmer knew that he had seen Fu Manchu, whose 'face was the living embodiment of Satan'.[47] This sounds suspiciously like the real-life Brilliant Chang, who did not arrive on the London scene until well after the war in 1922.

A 23-year-old West End taxi dancer named Freda Kempton had died from convulsions in her Paddington flat after swallowing cocaine. A Chinese restaurateur, known in the West End as Brilliant Chang, was arraigned in connection with her death. Unfortunately for Chang, it was life that imitated art rather than the other way around, and the newspapers were quick to

The Yellow Claw was first serialised in *Detective Story Magazine*, 1916

draw damning links between the dapper Chang and the fictitious Fu Manchu. *Daily Express* indictments of him as 'The Yellow King of the Dope Runners' drew immediate associations with Rohmer's evil brainchild and did nothing to help his case.

Literary historian Ross Forman suggests that *The Yellow Claw* may have been inspired by a wartime arrest related by Rohmer's friend Edward Tupper, organiser of the National Union of Seamen and a key proponent of anti-Chinese agitation. Tupper writes in his memoir, *Seaman's Torch*, of a conversation during the war with a police officer about a Chinese man who had been fined a hefty £300 (equivalent to £16 700 in 2013)[48] for opium possession:

Chief-Inspector Yeo – whom I knew very well, and whom I had helped to run to earth several undesirables – declared that this yellow man was merely the agent of a rich syndicate in England. This syndicate was distributing opium and its deadly derivatives throughout the West End; young officers, young women, and middle-aged men, racked by the nervous strain of war, were learning to 'kiss the cup' – smoke opium. In this was a threat against national life which might, in the long run, bring about a more devastating state of affairs than even the loss of the War could bring.[49]

The opium-related arrest may well be true although the fine sounds exaggerated. In July 1917, *The Times* reported the arrest of Ching Foo Jack and four other Chinese men discovered in a den in Poplar High Street, just east of Limehouse Causeway, cutting and weighing opium for sale. Ching was fined a total of £10, considerably less than the amount Tupper reported.[50] These arrests had become commonplace after Defence of the Realm Act (DORA) 40B came into force in 1916. DORA had been widened to criminalise the possession and sale of opium and cocaine. Tupper's recollection reads like a retrospective recycling of Rohmer's fictional scenarios. Either way, it demonstrates the circulation of anti-yellow conspiracy theories and tales of drug-fuelled depravity that would continue well after the Armistice.

Meanwhile, readers devoured stories of decadence and degeneracy among their betters. Rohmer's depiction of The Cave of the Golden Dragon, Mr King's 'opium-den deluxe' secreted in a basement crypt adjacent to Kan-Suh Concessions' wharfside warehouse, is frequented by 'none other than Sir Brian Malpas – the brilliant politician whom his leaders' had 'earmarked for office in the next cabinet'. Those who 'seek the solace of the brass pipe', we are told, include 'the most famous artistic folk of London; not only painters, but authors, composers, actors, actresses'; even 'the peerage, male and female, is represented'. Connections with actual

China are underscored. It turns out Sir Brian has 'lived for some time in China at the British legation – he curses the day he was 'appointed to Pekin'.[51]

It is in *The Yellow Claw* that Rohmer first orientalises Limehouse and highlights the presence of an actual Chinatown, small though it is. The point would not have been lost on his readers that this is an actual invasion, no less real than the Norman conquest of England in 1066. After the police raid on the premises of the Cave of the Golden Dragon, it is discovered of the building's origins that 'the pillars are . . . of a very early Norman pattern . . . I tell you it's the crypt of some old forgotten Norman church or monastery chapel'. A legend is revealed 'of the existence of a very large Carmelite monastery, accommodating over two hundred brothers, which stood somewhere adjoining the Thames within the area now covered by Limehouse Causeway and Pennyfields'.[52]

Rohmer and his readers were of a generation raised on school textbooks in which they were assured of England's imperial righteousness by explanations of English history in terms of successful, but crucially white, assimilations. As W. Locke so exemplifies:

I dare say every one of our forefathers, when they saw the Romans come first, were discouraged and thought . . . they should never be happy any more . . . But these very things were meant for their good. Their savage customs and barbarous manner of life were thus changed. There we find the first step on the ladder that has conducted Englishmen to such power and greatness . . . let us heartily thank God for it.[53]

Joseph Conrad's novella *Heart of Darkness* revisits this history too, albeit to rather different ends, exposing European imperialist culpability in an indictment narrated aboard the Nellie anchored near Gravesend, just downstream from Limehouse:

> But darkness was here yesterday. Imagine the feelings of a commander of a fine –what d'ye call 'em? – trireme in the Mediterranean, ordered suddenly to the north . . . Imagine him here – the very end of the world, a sea the color of lead, a sky the color of smoke, a kind of ship about as rigid as a concertina – and going up this river with stores, or orders, or what you like. Sandbanks, marshes, forests, savages, – precious little to eat fit for a civilized man, nothing but Thames water to drink.[54]

England's seemingly unshakeable imperial predominance was being questioned. Zeppelins rained bombs on London, but the threat of conquest by the Bosch was as nothing compared to that of the yellow races.

Rohmer would continue the theme in 1925 with *Yellow Shadows* published following the conviction of Brilliant

Chang the year before for cocaine trafficking. Loosely disguised as Burma Chang, the dope king paralleled *The Yellow Claw*'s Mr King, and his Limehouse residence was given a similar historic provenance:

> In Chinatown survive some few examples of country mansions, undevoured by the greedy maw of commercialism; for once, where dockland stretches its grimy fingers over the river bank . . . were broad meadows and prosperous farmsteads . . . Such a survival was the house of Burma Chang, its entrance a door in a long blank wall . . . this wall concealed a fine old manor which had known . . . many changes, none stranger than . . . the invasion of yellow settlers from China.[55]

In the aftermath of war, the resilience and endurance of Englishness was symbolised by the 'fine old manor house' in what amounts to a pastoral elegy of London's docklands. Yet at the same time, and articulated with certainty, the yellow invasion of England had begun.

Sinophilia

Thomas Burke was nothing if not idiosyncratic. While Sax Rohmer toed the establishment line with his unremittingly evil Chinamen whose interest in white women is part of their fiendish yellow plot to destroy the West, Burke followed *Limehouse Nights* (the notoriety of which had done him no harm at all, as it turned out) with an elegy for the vanished delights of pre-war Chinatown. Published in 1919, *Out and About: A Notebook of London in War-Time* guides the armchair tourist through London haunts both familiar and hidden. Burke is as ever the omniscient tour guide, seasoned habitué of dark side streets that lead 'to secret encampments of alien and outlaw'.[56] He is proud to boast he has 'clicked the chopsticks in Limehouse Causeway with the yellow boys'.[57]

In Nights in Town, the chapter 'A Chinese Night: Limehouse' presented the district as 'a spot to which one may escape from the banalities of the daily day'.[58] At that time, only encroaching public transport routes threatened to dilute the exclusivity of London's foreign quarters, and Limehouse had yet been spared the intrusion. *Out and About* mourns this pre-war Chinatown. Now, thanks to the unprecedented state control and excessive public surveillance initiated by DORA, 'Chinatown is a back number'. Where Rohmer blames 'the greedy maw of commercialism' for the very existence of dockland's grimy stretch, Burke accuses 'the commercial and controlled West' for suppressing what he describes as its 'dusky delicacies':

> You enter any bar and are at once under a cloud. Suspicion has been bred in all these docksmen by the cheap press. The patriotic stevedores regard you as a disguised alien. The landlord wonders whether you are one of those blasted newspapermen or are from the Yard.

Worst of all, DORA had 'khyboshed the little haunts that once invited to curious amusement'.[59] Wartime regulations imposed by DORA were introduced primarily to control sensitive information. Some would be retained into peacetime, including curfews on nightclub, restaurant, theatre and pub opening hours. The effect on the Chinese population of DORA's ban on opium smoking was to criminalise a large portion of it, giving the authorities a pretext to invade Chinese privacy, to stage exemplary deportations, and thereby to intimidate the entire community. Most significantly, as Marek Kohn

A Limehouse restaurant, 1920

points out, by placing the pleasures of nightlife outside the law, DORA created a drug 'scene'.[60] With drug legislation, the possibilities of Chinatown may have been dissipated but its symbolic role was intensified. Why, lamented *The Athenaeum*'s review of *Out And About*,

> do so many writers, in describing a beloved country or city adopt the elegiac tone? . . . is there no place left we can read about and fly to find more marvellous than ever? It would be delightful to believe the London of five years ago, mourned for so entertainingly by Mr Thomas Burke, would return now the war is over.[61]

Burke took a diametrically different standpoint to Rohmer. In the chapter 'Chinatown Revisited' he invokes the 'the soul of the Orient' to reflect upon the inadequacies of an industrialised, state-controlled West. Whilst civil liberties were being increasingly curtailed by the stringencies of DORA, Burke conjures the exotic reek of Limehouse in the 1890s, a nostalgic *mélange* of 'betel nut, chandu [opium] and fried fish', and its cosmopolitan clamour, a chorus of Cockney organ grinders, Salvation army bands and 'the rasp of a gramophone delivering records of interminable Chinese dramas'.[62] Burke's stories did not deny the public their worst imaginings of unbridled miscegenation and substance abuse among the lower orders, yet his Chinatown writing was in large part inspired by the exoticism of fin-de-siècle decadence. This embrace of all things Chinese allies him with an altogether more highbrow set of Sinophiles, chief among them the American modernist poet Ezra Pound.

In the years before the war, a growing intellectual vogue for an exotic and antiquated China was a constituent element of London's avant-garde quest for artistic renewal. There was a desire for new modes of representation that might give expression to a sense of cultural crisis. Those artists and writers who would be so roundly attacked by those who saw the war as an opportunity to cleanse the culture of foreign influence embraced the teachings and cultures of the East as an alternative to the discredited and outmoded certainties of their Victorian forebears.

A significant landmark in the Edwardian positioning of a modernist aesthetic was the opening in June 1910 of the British Museum's Exhibition of Chinese and Japanese Painting curated by erstwhile Decadent poet Laurence Binyon, keeper of oriental prints and drawings at the museum. Ezra Pound had been introduced to Binyon not long after arriving in London in the autumn of 1908. Binyon had just published *Painting in the Far East* and Pound attended his lecture series on 'Art and Thought in East and West', remarking them in a letter home as 'intensely interesting'.[63] The flamboyantly attired and outlandishly coiffured young poet, eager to make his mark on London's literary scene, would join Binyon and his coterie of connoisseurs during lunch hours at the Vienna Café in Oxford Street. Their talk would prepare the ground for Pound's adoption of what he conceived as the principles of a Chinese aesthetic to be. Bohemian literary hostess Brigit Patmore would later recall of the period that 'unaware of the approaching disasters of the First World War, a wave of creative activity seemed to be sweeping London […] Ezra's driving force was everywhere.'[64]

London's cultural landscape with Pound as its lynchpin was broadened by artistic interaction with things Chinese. Excited by the compact concision of the Chinese ideogram, Pound developed the poetic creed of Imagism, a pared down and fragmentary poetic style, as a means of escaping the heavy legacy of what he dismissed as Victorian poetical slither. 'There is *no* long poem in Chinese', he wrote in excitement to Dorothy Shakespear (his future wife) in October 1913. 'They hold if a man can't say what he wants to in 12 lines, he'd better leave it unsaid. THE period was 4th cent. B.C. – Chu Yüan, Imagiste.'[65] Pound's theory of the Vortex (which underpinned London's avant-garde movement, Vorticism) was based on his understanding of the etymological nature of the Chinese ideogram: 'It is a radiant node or cluster; it is what I can, and must perforce, call a VORTEX, from which, and through which, and into which, ideas are constantly rushing.'[66] Here Pound acknowledged Binyon's inventiveness in 'extending the borders of occidental knowledge', a sentiment he communicated in a letter to John Quinn, a New York lawyer and modernist art patron, stating unequivocally that he 'should like to see China replace Greece as the body of antiquity.'[67]

London's young modernists invented themselves in terms of generational conflict: 'We will sweep out the past century', Ezra Pound proclaimed in *BLAST 1*, published in July 1914, concurrent with the outbreak of war. Other young poets continued to rail against their elders throughout the war years. Robert Graves promised in 1915 that when the war was over he would 'try to root out more effectively the more obnoxious survivals of

Victorianism' while Wilfred Owen wrote to his mother in 1917: 'The Victoria Cross! I covet it not. Is it not Victorian? Yah! Pah!'[68]

Burke himself held an ambivalent position with regard to modernism. His own evocation of the Orient was a means of articulating nostalgia for the losses of the pre-war period, for bygone freedoms both political and social:

> I feel if ever there was an age when at the same time the individual was crushed and the masses chained to fetishes and slogans, it is now. If ever there was an age when unpleasant things were hushed up, or ignored, or made to appear pleasant, it is this . . . do not pretend that you are footloose and free, and that the Victorians were shackled.[69]

For Burke, the war was an excuse for increased state intervention with its drink and drug laws, rationings, bad beer, passports and curfews. In the preface to *Nights in Town* he had written:

> These chapters on London life deal almost exclusively with the period before war, when the citizen was permitted to live in freedom, to develop himself to his finest possibilities, and to pursue happiness as he was meant to do. Since the delights of these happy times have been

taken from us, perhaps never to be restored, it is well that they should be recorded before they are forgotten.

As he described it later, the period that spanned the war was a 'spasm of labour between the old and the new', between the Decadence of Aubrey Beardsley and Wilde, and the post-war period of the vacuous, party-manic, mindlessly hedonistic twenties.[70] Along with personal freedoms, the vibrant artistic culture that had sprung up immediately before the war was suppressed, its maelstrom of 'isms – Aestheticism, Cubism, Futurism, Vorticism, etc. – constituted a common enemy that threatened the moral foundations of the nation. As we see in *The Yellow Claw*, public opinion in England held that the war against Germany was a war against modernism

'Getting orient from all quarters'

– Ezra Pound, 1913

In 1913, Ezra Pound had written to his future wife Dorothy Shakespear that he was 'getting orient from all quarters'.[71] He had dined in 'a new curious and excellent restaurant chinois' and had been doing 'shows *chinesques*'. The restaurant is probably the one described by Burke in *Out and About* as 'the Chinese café in Regent Street' which, in spite of wartime restrictions, continued to 'furnish for the adventurous stomach such trifles as black eggs (guaranteed thirty years old), shark's fin at seven shillings a portion, stewed seaweed, bamboo shoots and sweet birds' nests'.[72]

Arguably, 1913 was the year in which the consumption of Chinese exoticism became aestheticised in displays of cutting-edge chic. It was the same year that the writer Katherine Mansfield, 'looking very pretty in a Chinese costume', introduced the acts at The Cave of The Golden Calf, Madame Frida Strindberg's newly opened Cabaret Theatre Club, down a small cul-de-sac off Regent Street.[73] Pound's co-conspirator on *BLAST*, Wyndham Lewis, devised a Chinese shadow play, *Ombres Chinoises*, which was performed in October at the club, an evening that Ford Madox Ford would fictionalise after the war in his novel *The Marsden Case*. The novel's protagonist is commissioned to 'write a shadow play to brighten London and help a young designer who wanted a little advertisement before wealthy London types'.[74] Ford would memorialise The Cave of the Golden Calf as a place to which all London wished to belong, 'a cavern below ground where dim and uncommented on things happened' and where 'everything was so foreign and so oriental.'[75]

Ford's is a wistful evocation of the cosmopolitan social scene of London's pre-war avant-garde. In the conservative moral climate of wartime, the brief cultural flowering that had come to dynamic fruition in Madame Strindberg's nightclub was the epitome of everything that was wrong with England. The basement premises were decorated with Jacob Epstein's hieratic sculptures, and paintings by Wyndham Lewis and Spencer Gore that pulsed with discordant colour; the whole conceived in a shameless emulation of the wild pagan rites of the biblical cult of the Golden Calf, the graven idol worshipped by the dissident Israelites. It was Epstein's work that took much of the brunt of moralist concern, generally expressed in distinctly racial terms: 'the aesthetic tendencies of the most advanced school of modern art are leading us back to the primitive instincts of the savage', worried *The Connoisseur*.[76] Epstein's radical turn from the conventions of classical Greek and Roman sculpture to the aesthetic traditions of the East continued to draw attack for decades to come, not least for his choice of ethnically diverse models, branded 'semi-Oriental sluts' by one newspaper.[77]

On any given night, the Cabaret Theatre Club programme might juxtapose a Hungarian Gypsy band with African-American ragtime, a Salome veil dance with Argentinean tango. Its eclectic mix of a declared 'intelligent revelry' delighted some and horrified many – hence the police raids that would follow.

In *The Yellow Claw*, Sax Rohmer would echo the popular press and lampoon the club's clientele of

'Cubists, Voo-dooists, Futurists and other Boomists'.[78] This is the crowd who flock to the private view of Olaf van Noord, 'the god of the Soho futurists' and painter of 'the weirdest nightmares imaginable'. 'Our Lady of the Poppies' is the blasphemous title of an artwork for which a Eurasian woman, Mahara, is the model. Her figure has a 'devilish and evil grace' and the work on display is 'lunatic'. The artist van Noord, his hair worn long and brushed back, wafts an opium-filled cigarette in a long amber holder. A little Negro boy proffers thimble-sized cups of Chinese tea. A bewildered journalist wonders how to 'notice the thing seriously? Personally I am writing it up as a practical joke! . . . I can't see how to handle it except as funny stuff'.[79]

The onset of the war signified a return to an insular suspicion of foreigners. While there is no mention of the war itself in *The Yellow Claw*, it presents a picture of England infected with a European disease that has caused it to become degenerate and open to Asiatic corruption. The disease is modernism, an infection bred in the 1890s.

At the same time that Rohmer and the press played to the public's xenophobic nightmares, Pound was pioneering a new appreciation for Chinese modes of artistic representation. As soon as war was declared, he wrote home to reassure his parents back in Hailey, Idaho that London was 'not yet dynamited by the

Deutschers' and that he had begun to work on some Chinese poetry.[80] Through his connection with Binyon, Pound had been given a set of notes by the widow of orientalist scholar Ernest Fenollosa. They were English cribs of a number of Tang Dynasty poems by Li Po. When Pound began working from the notebooks, he had absolutely no knowledge of the Chinese language and little of the textual or cultural conventions of Chinese poetry. However, what he read in Fenollosa's notes tallied uncannily with his own ideas about modern poetry, expressed in his formulations of Imagism and Vorticism. In the face of Filippo Tommaso Marinetti's domineering promotion of Futurism, a competing modernist art movement that embraced dynamism and technology into its artistic doctrine, Pound had been equally relentless in his promotion of a Chinese-based aesthetic of Imagist poetry and Vorticist sculpture. Reviewing an exhibition at Regent Street's Goupil Gallery for *The Egoist* in the spring of 1914, he compared the spirit of Henri Gaudier Brzeska's sculptures 'to bronzes of China's Zhou Dynasty (1046 BC–256 BC), the era that produced Confucius, Mencius, Laozi, and other great sages'.

As Pound set to work on the translations, his young protégé Gaudier-Brzeska was writing battle reports from trenches 'a foot deep in liquid mud' for the second issue of Pound's Vorticist journal *BLAST*.[81] In return Pound sent him the fifth-century Chinese poems 'Song of the Bowmen of Shu' and 'Lament of the Frontier Guard'. 'They depict our situation in a wonderful way', Gaudier wrote back. Pound's selection of fourteen poems from the 150 or so in the notebooks were published in April 1915, titled *Cathay*. Gaudier wrote to him from the Marne: 'I keep the book in my pocket. Indeed I use [the poems] to put courage in my fellows.[82] Gaudier-Brzeska's 'Vortex (Report from the Trenches)' appeared in *BLAST 2* in July, poignantly appended by his obituary.[83]

Cathay was widely praised. W. B. Yeats applauded its 'freshness, elegance and simplicity' and T. S. Eliot described Pound as the 'inventor of Chinese poetry for our time'.[84] The poems about exiled warriors and sorrowing wives in ancient China drew unmistakable parallels with the slaughter and embattled stalemate of Europe in 1915:

> In both there were barbarians to be fought off [and] soldiers having a hard time at the front; in both there was a lack of enlightened direction from the ruling class at home; and in both the arts, including the art of government, were in their usual decadent state'.[85]

When Ford wrote from the battlefront offering support for *Limehouse Nights* in the face of possible censorship from the major libraries, his encouragement took the form of an ancient Chinese proverb. This proverb had stood him in good stead, he assured Burke, when he'd been losing money on the *English Review*: 'when I have been robbed, misquoted, slandered or blackmailed, I have always just shrugged my shoulders and murmured that it would be hypocrisy to seek for the person of the Sacred Emperor in a low tea-shop'.[86] Ford would return to the proverb in 1919 for Gaudier-Breszka's obituary essay, 'Henri-Gaudier-Brzeska: The Story of a Low Tea-Shop'. Here he describes how his first encounter with the handsome young sculptor in fact confounded that proverb: 'in an underground restaurant, the worst type of thieves' kitchen – those words rose to my lips'. In bohemian London before the war, 'in appalling exhibitions, in nasty nightclubs, in dirty restaurants' (a rather backhanded compliment to Madame Strindberg),

> one would be stopped for a moment, in the course of a sentence, by the glimpse of a brutal chunk of rock that seemed to have lately fallen unwanted from a slate quarry, or, in the alternative by a little piece of marble that seemed to have the tightened softness of the haunches of a faun.[87]

The debates and developments both artistic and social introduced by the modernist encounter with Chinese things would incubate during the war, but Ford's marvellous elegy stands for something irretrievably gone. The genius of a little netsuke by Gaudier or the blissful brutalities of Epstein's savage totems – this was the shock of the new – the Sacred Emperor, albeit briefly, discovered in a low tea-shop.

Chu Chin Chow: 'More Navel than Millinery'

In December 1917, a production of the perennial 'Chinese' favourite *Aladdin* at Drury Lane opened to reviews that were more than usually enthusiastic for a seasonal pantomime. The appetite for theatrical entertainment had never been so insatiable as London audiences swelled with troops passing through on their way to the front or returning on leave and craving escapism from the horrors of battle. The restrained delicacy of *Aladdin's* scenes was hailed as 'artistic' by *The Globe*. The reviewer commended Drury Lane, that bastion of Victorian grand pantomime, for having broken with vulgar dazzle and in doing so to have 'ended the long march towards the ideal pantomime'.[88] *The Pall Mall Gazette* cheered its 'complete divorce from the rough-and-ready music-hall element' of Victorian pantomime: '*Aladdin* is as *Aladdin* should be, a piece of conscientious *chinoiserie* always'.[89]

Pantomime, historically, is a form of entertainment cobbled together by generations of theatre managers in search of an audience. The scripts, with their contemporary slang and topical allusion, offer us an informative guide to events that have stirred the public imagination, from major political crises to everyday trivia. The Chinese setting of *Aladdin*, gorgeous in its timeless antiquity and ridiculous in the antiquated antics of the Widow Twankey, the clowning Chinese laundrymen, etc., had endured more than a century of changing attitudes towards China. Yet at the same time, the endurance of British pantomime as a tradition has always been its capacity for adapting to new trends.

In the years leading up to the war, pantomime's process of modification led to the absorption of the hugely popular Broadway revue. Fast-moving, light and frothy, revues were themed shows that combined the most up-to-date dance and music styles (then the tango and American ragtime songs) with short sketches offering witty dissections of popular fads or celebrities of the day. The primary attraction of revue for soldiers, of course, was its scenic display of the newly fashionable, streamlined female body.

The popularity of Drury Lane's stylised *Aladdin* lay in its reflection of the contemporary taste for revue and its similarity to *Chu Chin Chow*, a revue that had opened at Her Majesty's Theatre the previous summer. *Chu Chin Chow* was proving unstoppable, the runaway theatrical hit of the war. *The Morning Post*, while enthusing over *Aladdin*'s shimmering curtain of crystal drops that rose to reveal two imposing mandarin narrators, remarked of the Emperor of China: he is 'almost as overpowering and resonant a Celestial as Mr Oscar Asche in *Chu Chin Chow* an entertainment of which one is frequently reminded'.[90] *The Stage* noted technical as well as stylistic borrowings from that show: 'the hero's adventures are foreshadowed by means of fleeting pictures coming and going iris-wise, for a kind of contractile diaphragm is used as in *Chu Chin Chow*.[91]

The show was produced by the stage actor and impresario Oscar Asche. He based it on the pantomime favourite *Ali Baba and the Forty Thieves* and designated it an 'Eastern revue', transforming the main character into a 'Chinese' man and naming the show after him. Asche himself played the wily leader of the robber band – really Abu Hasan, the leader of the forty thieves – who, disguised as a Shanghai merchant complete with silken skullcap, black pigtail, long claw-like fingernails and even longer moustaches, calls himself Chu Chin Chow.[92] It is not difficult to see the resonances between Chu Chin Chow and Fu Manchu. Photographs of Asche's costume and the illustrated posters for the show make the link explicit.

Nothing quite like *Chu Chin Chow* had been seen on the London stage before. It was the acme of decades of orientalist theatrical fantasy with its spectacular scenery and parades of exotically costumed girls. *Chu Chin Chow* captured the spirit of the age: 'Mr Asche's . . . excursion into the region of fantastic, polyphonic, polychromatic orientalism', expounded 'is a kaleidoscope series of scenes, now romantic, now realistic, now Futurist or Vorticist, but always beautiful.'[93]

Like Rohmer's presentation of Chinese Limehouse, *Chu Chin Chow* gave its wartime audience an Orient endorsed by consensual ideology. In this case it was the tradition of late-Victorian imperialism blended with the sexual frivolity of Edwardian musical comedy in which chorus girls in cartwheel hats were whisked off by gents in safari helmets to colonial outposts with names like

Queuing outside Her Majesty's Theatre

Oscar Asche as the devilish
Chu Chin Chow

Pynka Pong or Ylang Ylang. At the turn of the century,
audiences were fed on a diet of their own imperial
supremacy in shows such as *San Toy* (1899), *A Chinese
Honeymoon* (1901), *The New Aladdin* (1906) and *See
See* (1906). These were characterised by ridiculous
dialogue and outlandish scenarios and provided a space
in which taboos of class, race and sexuality could be
played out.

Chinoiserie musical comedy always revolved around
an interracial romance. One of the strengths of popular
culture, as historian Robert Bickers observes, lies in its
ability to entrench social attitudes by imaginatively flout-
ing them. Central to actual Sino-British relationships
was the necessity of maintaining sexual distance between
British and Chinese.[94] This was suspended on stage as
stars like Lily Elsie or Gabrielle Ray, looking gorgeous

in Chinese costume, fluttered their fans and flirted. Needless to say, however daring and modern the shows may have seemed, interracial love plots were strictly one-way traffic, gallant English chap falls for blushing 'Chinese' maiden, never the other way around. And even while allowing that the China of musical comedy was fine as frivolous fun, reviewers seldom failed to remind audiences of the reality of China and Chinese people. George Edwardes' legendary Gaiety Theatre, now recognised for having been a major influence on the modern musical comedy, was reviewed in one such instance:

> I should not expect anyone who knows his Far East . . . to be hypnotised by the glamour of Mr Edwardes' . . . The fact is that – people, life, costumes, morals – China is absolutely the most sordid and most sombre country under the sun – the one corner of the earth's face which one never catches a smile upon.[95]

Chu Chin Chow, a combination of Victorian panto-mime, Edwardian musical comedy and American revue, resulted in a show that was to become a first port of call for troops on leave. They were often given only twenty-four hours and, not unexpectedly, were determined to have a good time. *Chu Chin Chow* followed in the long-established English tradition that an oriental theme, be it harem, bathhouse or slave market, gave theatrical audiences a licence to gaze at the exposed flesh of white women.

If the wartime allies filling London were not always competent enough in English to handle sophisticated verbal banter, they could appreciate the bare midriffs of beautiful slave girls. *Chu Chin Chow*'s ever evolving costume parade was designed to reveal as much skin as possible. As Herbert Beerbohm Tree, manager of Her Majesty's Theatre, famously quipped, there was 'more navel than millinery'.[96] One costume design, a skin-coloured body stocking complete with fuzzy Afro wig, went so far as to designate a Nile dancer as 'nude'. The *Daily Mirror* got away with a saucy shot of four 'Desert dancers', bizarrely clad in Viking horns and bits of leopard skin, by asking its readers: 'Do these dresses offend you?'[97] In terms of any relation to authenticity, geographic or historical, the answer might well have been – yes.

'Silk-legged hordes'

The upheaval in social conditions caused by the war played a formative part in the increasingly sexualised content of theatrical productions. While rules and regulations tightened up in other walks of life, there was increased laxity in regard to the theatre. The legacy of Victorian finance capitalism passed on to the twentieth-century London stage had been the need to minimise

A revealing *Chu Chin Chow* pagoda dress costume

risk and maximise profit. In hindsight it was observed that 'financial speculators settled on the theatre like a cloud taking advantage of its vulnerability and the care-lessness it displayed about its reputation in those hectic four or five years'.[98] From the start of the war, licence to present what the Lord Chancellor might previously have condemned as lewd, suggestive or salacious resulted in a slew of bedroom farce and pyjama plays. This liber-tinism reflected what was going on offstage. London, already encroached upon by legions of young women, the 'silk-legged hordes' as D. H. Lawrence dubbed the newly independent typists and telephonists, was now inundated with servicemen.[99] Other young women abandoned domestic service for munitions factories and vastly increased their wages.

Previous modes of behaviour were abandoned in the social chaos provoked by the war. Soldiers 'hot from the trenches or straight from the Colonies thought that they were perfectly justified by being soldiers in throwing overboard every moral, social and marital tie, in order to have a rousing time' observed one commentator.[100] What was worse, they were encouraged by women, Lawrence's 'bare-armed swarms' that 'buzz around the coloured lights of pleasure'.[101] By the end of 1916, the exploitation of an unparalleled wave of sexual freedom had become a predominating theatrical feature.

Chu Chin Chow was a paradox in that it offered a few hours' escape from the war yet was very much a part of it. Its storyline of 'heroism and ingenuity . . . of winning against the odds bought into the romanticised jingoism of the nation's endeavours on the killing fields'.[102] Mythological tales abounded of the show's effect on national consciousness. Men brought recorded discs back to France with them and sent home snaps of concert parties in coolie hats performing *Chu Chin Chow* at the front, and even in a German POW camp, in drag. It was rumoured that when the first detachment of victorious troops marched into Germany, the military band played the 'Robbers' March' from *Chu Chin Chow*. During the course of its run, profits from the sale of merchandise were donated to the war effort to fund field hospitals and canteens for the troops. The production survived numerous interruptions from air raids and electricity cuts as well as sundry mishaps such as the death of a camel, reputedly killed when falling through some glass pavement lights into the cellar below. Its keeper warned Mr Asche not to eat out in Soho for a while; in the light of meat rationing, he had sold the carcass to a local restaurant owner.

In true pantomime tradition, the show commented on real events outside the theatre and was adjusted to fit the course of the war. *Chu Chin Chow* moved from being light relief from the horrors of war to become a 'defining theatrical chronicler of the war.'[103] The script evolved to include topical news developments while at the same time each new scene was chiefly motivated by its ability to engineer an excuse for another costume overhaul and even greater exposure of flesh. And just as keen on the show as the sailors and Tommies were young women. A new species had emerged, the so-called gallery girl, the flapper equivalent of the stage-door Johnny: 'in the War-time theatre . . . the ruler of the roost was the half-baked, over-heated flapper. Damn her . . . flappers in the stalls wanted to see flappers on the stage.'[104] And as indicated by a proliferation of public fancy-dress events and costume balls, young women wanted to act out their orientalist fantasies in the social sphere: 'These ladies in our picture', captioned a *Tatler* photo spread of *Chu Chin Chow*, 'are the leading mannequins from Baghdad, and their raiment, though very slightly different from some of the latest Paris models might perhaps create a sensation if it was seen on this side instead of the curtain side of the footlights.'[105]

Not everyone was enamoured of the show. One critic sneered that the soldiers gladly went back to the trenches to escape it and Thomas Burke concurred with this.[106] In *Out And About* he dismissed the show with the comment: 'Her Majesty's Theatre is 'running a pantomime . . . knowing that the boys on leave are not likely to be too hypercritical, the theatrical money-lords . . . have taken advantage of the situation to fob us of with any old store-room rubbish.'[107] Unsurprisingly, other shows with a Chinese theme attempted to cash in on the success of *Chu Chin Chow*. In addition to *Aladdin*, Drury Lane plumped for American publisher and composer Isidore Witmark's *Shanghai*. This was an operetta that combined an American-style musical with exotic scenes in a Shanghai temple and on board a Chinese junk. Spectacular but unmemorable was the general response.

The taste for an exotically staged Orient and villainous stage-Chinamen had predated the war and would long outlast it. *Chu Chin Chow* had been the smash hit of World War One and the longest running stage show until it finally ended in 1922. By that time, the combined portraits of the Chinese in popular fiction, criminal reality and press sensation would determine their representation on stage.

In the mid-1920s, a delegation of Chinese students concerned about the hostility of popular culture to Chinese people protested that no less than five plays currently showing in London's West End represented Chinese people in a 'vicious and objectionable form': *The Silent House, Hit the Deck, The Yellow Mask, Listeners* and *Tin Gods*. W. C. Ch'en (Chen Weicheng), the Chargé d'Affaires at the Chinese Legation, made an official complaint to the Foreign Office but to little avail. Speaking at a China Society anniversary dinner, Ch'en drew attention to this growing tendency in theatre and film productions in London, pointing out that 'No other Oriental nation is thus singled out for objectionable dramatic treatment so far as its people are concerned.'[108] He suggested that authors guilty of this might be fined £100. He was responded to by Sir Edward Crowe, Vice President of the Royal Society of Arts, who said by way of apology that surely Mr T. P. O'Connor, as 'a friend of China', would not pass anything untoward.[109] T. P. O'Connor had been appointed President of the British Board of Film Censors during the war. An ardent Irish nationalist, O'Connor was also a founding father of the popular press, starting up a handful of papers in the late 1890s. His famous 'list of 43' strictures, submitted to the Cinema Commission of Enquiry in 1917, pertained exhaustively to sex, drugs and blasphemy. Despite the severity of moral censorship, the closest the list came to a ban on derogatory representations of race was 'No. 20: Incidents having a tendency to disparage our Allies', and it is doubtful that this sanction was ever exercised on behalf of the Chinese.

Whilst distraction could be found in *Chu Chin Chow* for a war-wearied public, other kinds of escapism might be found after the show finished. To the indignation of a lobby led by *The Times,* London nightclubs persisted in staging attractions such as an Apache night or a bacchanalian revel, even distributing advertising fliers to officers. The home secretary responded with the Clubs Act, which imposed a midnight curfew on weekends with last orders at nine-thirty for restaurants, pubs and clubs. London was effectively shut down.

Some thirty years before in 1882, Robert Louis Stevenson had published a collection of stories titled *New Arabian Nights*, conjuring an oriental fairy tale of London's landscape after dark. Burke would later express that if Stevenson had been there to witness wartime London's after-dark goings-on, he 'could have placed it in a New Arabian Night which would have topped all the others in his stories of the extravagant and bizarre'. With wartime restrictions, London was 'a changeling . . . All outdoor lamps were painted blue, and all shop and house lights thickly screened. All public-houses were shut at half-past nine'. Burke's suggestive picture of the blue-lit City chimes with the orientalised landscape of Stevenson's London that had captured the popular imagination at the turn of the century. Now, only the lights of theatres and music halls glimmered through the 'blue mist'.[110]

But curfews only served to drive London's nightlife underground, where by all accounts it continued at more hectic a pace than ever: 'Entertainment and distraction of other sorts were held behind closed doors', remembered Burke as, despite attempts at regulation, cocaine-fuelled speakeasies and bottle parties proliferated.[111] By 1915, there were 150 illegal nightclubs in Soho alone. Leading socialite Lady Diana Manners described 'uproarious parties behind barred doors' held by her ever diminishing group of friends, 'called by our enemies the "Dances of Death"'.[112] Absinthe, vodka, chloroform and opium were their narcotics of choice – their enemies, the newspapers.

Hints of a vogue for drug-taking among the scions of the upper class surfaced in the gossip columns of the London press. The *Evening News* blamed a 'growing craze for opium smoking' in West End bohemia among dissolute flappers 'of the leisured class' from whom Britain's fighting men must be protected.[113] 'Women and Aliens Prey on Soldiers' and 'London in the Grip of The Drug Craze' were among the frantic headlines over the following months. Observations such as 'no one seems to know why the girls . . . find the drugs so easy to obtain' were disingenuous.[114] The spotlight was already trained on the Chinese in Limehouse, and with the increased media scrutiny, the authorities were pressured to respond. It was on 28 July 1916 that DORA 40B came into effect, outlawing the possession of cocaine or opium.

While doping was portrayed as a deadly menace to the war effort, for the Chinese seaman down in Limehouse, the mysterious vice of public speculation had always been a part of his daily routine: 'as unremarkable as lunch or breakfast' he would get up in the morning, smoke a pipe 'and then go off to work'.[115] Although the newspaper stories were largely apocryphal, repetition conveyed the impression that addiction spread by Chinese dealers was fast becoming a nationwide threat. The Chinese causeway in Limehouse, although geographically and culturally remote from the hub of the metropolis, would always haunt the West End and well beyond. The public would continue to be entertained by the Fu Manchu series until well after the end of the war, and no matter where his mysteries were set – whether they took place in England, the south of France or Egypt – Sax Rohmer would work in at least some mention of that dreadful district, London's Chinatown in Limehouse.

Aftermath: White Girls on Dope

Armistice with Germany on 11 October 1918 would signal the end of the war, and few occasions celebrating the milestone would be as spectacularly gorgeous as Oscar Asche's newly devised item in the third act of *Chu Chin Chow*. In a triumphant return to high-Victorian pantomime, a scene titled 'The Allies and the Dominions' was inserted into the show. A group of 'fair representatives' stood to attention modestly wrapped up in the flags of the participant countries: Belgium, New Zealand, Canada, Japan and India, to name a few.[116] India was represented by a blacked-up boy, a colonial 'child' of Britannia who was played by Asche's leading lady, Lily Brayton. Any awkwardness in having a white actress represent a black race was thus neatly avoided.

Notably absent from the roll call was China, despite the fact that she had joined the Allies in August 1917. Of course the real reason was that the success of the show was in large part due to the magnetic and perfidious

Chu the Chinaman, and the inclusion of China among the heroes would have been difficult to reconcile.

How aware the British public were of China's part in the war one can only surmise. As Mark O'Neill points out in *The Chinese Labour Corps*, the recruitment of a 135000-strong Chinese Labour Corps to the allied battlefront, beginning in July 1916, was a plan that had been kept secret, as British trade unions vehemently opposed the import of Chinese labour, wartime or not. In September 1916, the Trades Union Congress had commandeered newspaper headlines across the country with dramatic accusations of Chinese opium trafficking and the takeover of British maritime jobs.

In demanding that the government immediately introduce a bill to halt the increase in employment of Chinese labour on British ships, the unions asserted that this was 'almost as important a matter as the war'.[117] The leader of the National Union of Ships' Stewards, Cooks, Butchers and Bakers, complained that 'over 15,000 Chinese were engaged in British ships' but there was no suggestion of how these crucial jobs might be filled. It was mooted that 'the present war having proved the necessity for a large number of men of British birth available for the manning of the British Navy and Mercantile Marine, it is necessary that every encouragement be given to boys of British birth to enter seafaring trades'. The issue of how to win the war was skirted. Inevitably, conditions in England's Chinatowns were raised. It was claimed that more than 4000 Chinese were 'living in Liverpool in places such as no boarding-house or lodging-house keeper should be allowed to keep' and that of even more astounding a character were the opium dens and gaming houses in East London where opium was being manufactured in large quantities and smuggled overseas. Mr March, on behalf of the Limehouse-adjacent borough of Poplar, was a lone voice in attempting to defend these accusations, stating that only one such case had in fact been discovered.[118]

He was no match for the outspoken James Sexton, who said the Aliens Act 1905, which had been followed

The Trades Union Congress aggressively campaigned against the import of Chinese labour in nationally circulated newspapers by the much tougher Aliens Restriction Act 1914, had proved a fraud. Sexton had raised the commission of enquiry into the Liverpool Chinese community in 1906 to draw public attention to 'this horrible state of affairs'. Sexton claimed Chinese were 'the most dangerous of all aliens', selling their wives and daughters before leaving their own country to ship as crew 'at a shilling a month'.[119]

The Chinese did not take this slander quietly. A spirited letter from 'the leading Chinamen of Liverpool' was published in the paper the following week. The letter contested the figure of 4000 Chinese resident in Liverpool, stating there were no more than 4000 Chinese across the country and besides 'our opponents say nothing of the 20,000 or 30,000 Britishers who are occupying good positions and enjoying peaceful dwellings in China and who do not want to come home'. Sexton's commission of 1906 was referred to, which had entirely refuted accusations of insanitary boarding houses in Liverpool's Chinese quarter. The letter was also a defence against the charges of opium trafficking: 'Who first forced opium into our country against our wish and will and made us poor as a nation? . . . The truth is opium is now entirely stopped, as our critics ought to know, both in London, Liverpool, Cardiff and everywhere else, and Chinese have bid farewell to the habit'.

Chinese seamen were employed because ship own-ers found them steady and reliable and 'to get Britishers to work on ships is almost impossible, unless it is they cannot work on land'.

The letter concluded by asking that Sexton 'and all other slanderers feel thoroughly ashamed of themselves for insulting a class of people who have never harmed them but give proof after proof of their friendship towards Great Britain and her Allies'.[120]

In 1919, the Aliens Act would once again be amended to extend the wartime emergency powers. The Aliens Restriction Act of 1919 made further restrictions con-cerning the employment of alien seamen aboard British merchant ships. Chinese seamen were caught up in the act's provisions but, in the interests of commerce, the act made certain allowances: 'where the Board of Trade are satisfied that aliens of any particular race (other than for-mer enemy aliens) are habitually employed afloat in any capacity, or in any climate for which they are specifically fitted, nothing in this section shall prejudice the right of aliens of such race to be employed on British ships'.

One might argue of Asche's omission of China in the 'victory' scene that her role was non-combatant, but the same could be said of Japan, and Japan was included. Of course, Japan was a country to be taken seriously whereas China was not. After the surprising defeat of Russia in the Russo-Japanese War of 1905, the problem of how to treat a yellow nation as an equal partner had required ingenious thinking. Previous anthropological calculations that had emphasised the degeneracy of oriental races were adjusted and phrenological similarities discovered between the Japanese and Aryan physiology: 'one curious similarity runs through the whole, that is, the striking similarity between Japs and our own people. This resemblance manifests itself in manner, physical stamp and shape of head'.[121] This indicated 'considerable mental power' and constituted a 'good augury for the growth of sympathy between east and west.' Politicians and newspapermen were united in singing the praises of the Japanese. In private, opinion was different. G. K. Chesterton recorded a conversation with Winston Churchill and Charles Masterman, head of the British War Propaganda Bureau, in which both voiced distrust of the Japanese as 'a species of Mongolian monkey who mimicked the Hun in materialism and militarism and who in the future would sweep civilisation off the earth'.[122]

Fashionable London followed the example of *Chu Chin Chow* and celebrated Armistice night with a costumed pageant of Allied nations at the Great Victory Ball held in the Royal Albert Hall. A cohort of society ladies and stage beauties was led by Lady Diana Manners as Britannia. This time the line-up did include China in the parade. It was an altogether more eclectic affair, though, featuring an Aubrey Beardsley drawing and *Chu Chin Chow's* leading lady Lily Brayton as Cleopatra. But the gossip columns would have rather stronger stuff to report of the Victory Ball than who was wearing what.

Dope: A Story of Chinatown and the Drug Traffic

Rohmer's wartime fiction had mapped the social terrain of the doper: Futurist art openings, Soho coffee shops, Bond Street antiques emporiums, exclusive yet socially egalitarian nightclubs where the peerage mixed with chorus girls. In *The Yellow Claw*, 'modern girl journalist' Miss Cumberly captures the bohemian scene in her articles, given such titles as 'Dinner in Soho' or 'Curiosities of the Café Royal'. She identifies the corpse of dope addict Mrs Vernon as the 'girl who attended the most recent Art ball attired in a most monstrous Chinese costume, she belonged to a smart Bohemian set . . . burnt the candle at both ends; late dances, night-clubs, bridge parties, and other feverish pursuits'.[123]

The story of Billie Carleton, a young revue starlet who had died from a drugs overdose shortly after spending the evening at the Victory Ball, would become an international sensation that confirmed every aspect of England's wartime Yellow Peril propaganda. Headlines reached far and wide: 'Pretty Billie Carleton's Death

Has Led to Revelations of London Night Dissipations which Startled All England and Stirred the Police to Clean Up the Plague Spots of the British Capital'.[124] As investigations got underway they uncovered rampant recreational drug use within London's artistic circles and linked pyjama parties in Mayfair to dingy dwellings in dockside Chinatown. The inquest led to the prosecution of Ada Lau Ping, the Scottish wife of Limehouse resident Lau Ping You. She was accused of presiding over 'the unholy rites' of a circle of degenerates, supplying them with cocaine and opium, and 'cooking' for them at 'disgusting orgies' in the West End and opium debauches at her house in Limehouse Causeway.[125] In the manner in which they were reported, the details of the case exactly resembled a Fu Manchu novel.

The real-life Billie Carleton was a chorus girl with at least one wealthy sugar daddy, a Savoy Court apartment on the Strand and a much gossiped about drug habit. The circumstances of her unfortunate demise were to furnish Rohmer with his definitive drug-scare story, *Dope: A Story of Chinatown and the Drug Traffic*, published in 1919. The dust wrapper proclaimed the book to be based on true-life circumstances. The 'ultra-smart and vicious set' depicted go in for 'every monstrosity from Buenos Aires, Port Said and Pekin . . .' Whatever the facts of the trade may have been, Rohmer mythologised them in his fictionalised version of the Carleton case, stating: 'That the Chinese receive stuff in the East End and that it's sold in the West End every constable in the force is well aware'.[126]

According to popular mythology, raw opium was smuggled into London's docks from Far Eastern ports by Chinese arch-criminals. The stuff was stored in underground riverside warehouses and distributed to the fashionable salons and nightclubs of Mayfair and Piccadilly. In *The Yellow Claw* this East End/West End connection is implicit, the name of Mr King's opulent Limehouse opium palace, 'The Cave of The Golden Dragon', a thinly veiled Cave of the Golden Calf.

English women in Rohmer's wartime fiction were innocent, weak-willed and neurotic, or if utterly depraved, then they were inevitably aristocratic. In *The Yellow Claw*, Mira Leroux's mouth 'twitched strangely; she was a nervous wreck'.[127] In *Dope,* fragile actress Rita Dresden, the drug-addicted protagonist, lives the kind of rackety, bohemian life that renders a girl vulnerable to Chinese wiles. Neurasthenic Rita and her best friend, society divorcée Mollie Gretna, oscillate between *chandu* parties in Mayfair and rather more daring out-ings to Limehouse, orchestrated by Lola Sin, serpentine wife of opium smuggler Sin Sin Wa. The young women get caught up in the circle of Sir Lucien Pyne, a man who has a penchant for oriental and other proclivities that strongly suggest he was modelled on the notorious occultist Aleister Crowley. The trio drive to Sin Sin Wa's

Limehouse opium rooms through East End streets 'lit by naphtha flares in whose smoky glares Jews and Jewesses, Poles, Swedes, Easterns, dagoes and half-castes moved feverishly'.

Rohmer's Chinese quarter, unlike the noisy, squalid throng of neighbouring Whitechapel, is as inscrutable and foreboding as its inhabitants:

Passing over the canal, the car swung to the right into West India Dock Road. The uproar of the commercial thoroughfares was left far behind. Dark, narrow streets and sinister-looking alleys lay right and left of them . . . In the dimly lighted doorway of a corner house the figure of a Chinaman showed as a motionless silhouette. 'Oh!' sighed Mollie Gretna rapturously, 'a Chinaman! I begin to feel deliciously sinful!'[128]

When they get to the house of Sin Sin Wa, Mollie chooses her couch because 'it has cushions which simply reek of oriental voluptuousness and cruelty. It reminds me of a delicious book I have been reading called *Musk, Hashish and Blood*.' Mollie's arcane reference is to a limited edition translation of a work of French fin-de-siècle orientalism. Its author had stated in the preface that it was not a book 'for perusal in young ladies seminaries'.[129]

In the year that *Dope* was published, three London stage productions used the Billie Carleton story as a theme: *Dope: A Melodrama* by Frank Price, *Drug Fiends* by Owen Jones and *The Girl Who Took Drugs* (aka *Soiled*) by Aimee Grattan Clynes. Shortly afterwards, *World Pictorial News* printed a series of stories about London's East End and the ever encroaching Yellow Peril. The rapacious public appetite for stories of flimsily clad flappers and dope-peddling Chinks was triggered by the aforementioned Brilliant Chang case.

Freda Kempton had first met Brilliant Chang in that same Chinese restaurant in Regent Street frequented by Ezra Pound, in which Chang's wealthy family had a share. Chang appeared to have a finger in many pies and had allegedly been Kempton's drug supplier. The restaurant had been her last port of call on the night of her death. However, Chang was not implicated in her murder, and after the trial he moved his operations from the smart surrounds of Regent Street to the dockside Shanghai Restaurant on Limehouse Causeway. As Marek Kohn observes, this turn of events no doubt 'appealed to the prevailing sense of racial tidiness'. In reality, Chang was 'an educated, bourgeois, Westernised playboy, gone to ground among sailors, shopkeepers and artisans'.[130] He would have been quite out of place among the seamen and merchant sailors who populated Limehouse. Given the post-war vulnerability of the East End community to police pressure, 'two of its distinctive cultural traits' being opium-smoking and gambling, it is unlikely that Chang's presence would have been welcome.[131]

Brilliant Chang's legal case was aggravated by the inevitable affinities drawn between Rohmer's evil mastermind and the suavely dressed Chinese businessman with his known underworld connections and proven seduction techniques. According to one report, 'half-a-dozen drug-frenzied women together joined him in wild orgies' in his 'intoxicatingly beautiful den of iniquity' above the Shanghai Restaurant.[132]

Eventually, the death of a drug-addicted former actress, Violet Payne, enabled the police to frame Chang, who was charged and sentenced to fourteen months in prison followed by deportation.

Following Freda Kempton's death, the *Evening News* ran a series of sensational investigations claiming that a man known as the 'Chinese dope king' controlled London's drug traffic through a network of young women, the kind precariously employed as manicurists, masseuses, usherettes and cloak room attendants in the hotels and nightclubs of the West End.[133] Yellow Peril reportage, as usual, blurred the boundaries between fact and fiction. Ten days before Kempton's death, the paper had run a story elaborating on one of Rohmer's stock-in-trade scenarios in which actresses and fashionable women were said to acquire their drugs through shady antique shops in Holborn and Kensington, signalled

The smooth and dapper Brilliant Chang

to initiates by the Chinese curios displayed in their windows.[134] Rohmer would complete the pernicious cycle of life and art, barely disguising Brilliant Chang as Burma Chang, 'the richest man in Chinatown' and the evil genius of his new novel, *Yellow Shadows*.

Broken Blossoms

London's Yellow Peril scares of the Great War put Chinese Limehouse on the map. Within a year of publication, *Limehouse Nights* had been picked up by Hollywood director D.W. Griffith, who paid £1000 for the film rights. Burke's Limehouse struck a responsive chord with American audiences familiar with the Chinatowns of New York and San Francisco and their depiction in pulp fiction. Griffith adapted one of the stories, 'The Chink and the Child', into the film B*roken Blossoms*. The film was released in 1919 and would set a precedent for the iconic imagery of Chinese Limehouse on film through the twenties and beyond.

Griffith merged two other *Limehouse Nights* stories, 'Gina of the Chinatown' and 'The Sign of the Lamp', in another film, *Dream Street*, in 1921. In the years following the war, visiting Americans, including Hollywood celebrities Mabel Normand, Dolores Del Rio and Charlie Chaplin, made Burke's Limehouse an essential stop on their London itinerary. In 1924, Thomas Cook's thriving travel business began to lay on charabanc trips, much to the annoyance of Limehouse residents. At a carefully stage-managed time, doors would burst open and Chinese hired hands, complete with pigtails, would chase each other down the street wielding cleavers.[135] Having always been relied upon for sensational copy, Limehouse now supported a mini tourist industry.

It became commonplace, after a couple of champagne cocktails, for West End revellers to go slumming it 'down Chinatown way'.[136] Noël Coward, who had known Billie Carleton, acknowledged her story as inspiration for his play *The Vortex*, a scandalous whirl of sexual promiscuity and dope addiction that was the *succès de scandale* of 1924. Arnold Bennett recounts in

Limehouse opium den scene in, *Broken Blossoms*, 1919

his journal his own giddy rounds of fashionable pursuits in those first years after the end of the war – dinners at the Savoy, first nights at the theatre, weekends on his yacht – and the requisite trip to Chinatown: 'It took us exactly fifteen minutes to drive there from Ciro's'.[137]

By the 1930s, the notoriety of Chinese Limehouse had waned. In 1913, the year Burke wrote 'The Chink and the Child', Pennyfields in Limehouse was almost entirely inhabited by Chinese.[138] By 1934, the Register of Electors showed that of twenty-seven houses listed in the street only one was inhabited by a Chinese family.[139] The combined pressures of the Aliens Restriction Acts, the effects of the Great Depression and the slump in international shipping trade were responsible for the decline. Chinatown's provisions stores, boarding houses and restaurants suffered because, as one observer succinctly put it, 'the resident Chinks live on the visiting Chinks.'[140]

Exacerbating the problem was an intensification of police action in 1928 regarding possible legal infringements related to opium use and cocaine smuggling. With the pretext of checking immigration status, a series of co-ordinated police raids were made on Home Office instructions to all Chinese boarding houses, laundries, restaurants and homes throughout the country.[141] In the mid-thirties, slum clearance schemes in Liverpool's Pitt Street area and in Limehouse Causeway and Pennyfields scheduled these neighbourhoods for demolition. A journalist reported on the impending destruction: 'They did not seem to regret that Chinatown was going to be pulled down, as long as nice housing apartment flats were put up in its place for them.'[142]

The Anglo-Chinese children born during the war years, many of them to deported fathers, were now of school-leaving age but saw no future in Limehouse: 'the boys find work hard to get, and the girls drift about the streets ostracised by white girls of their own age. They, and not the white wives, are the broken blossoms.'[143] Thomas Cook's suggested route for an 'East End Drive' no longer made an attraction of Limehouse.[144] The myth declined along with the reality. The occasional story about England's shrinking Chinatown communities would make the papers, but the only sympathy was for 'the sensational writer bereft of one of his more thrilling scenarios'.[145]

ACKNOWLEDGEMENTS

My thanks to Mike Tsang at Penguin China for commissioning this book and to Imogen Liu for her editing skills. Additional thanks to Pak Hung Chan for sharing his research on Liverpool's Chinatown. Images are from the author's own collection.

NOTES

1   George R. Sims, 'In Limehouse and the Isle of Dogs', Chapter 11, *Off the track in London* (London: Jarrold & Sons, 1911). Originally published in *The Strand*, July 1905.

2   See Jerry White, *Zeppelin Nights: London in the First World War* (London: The Bodley Head, 1914), p. 82. The figure is from *HC Debates*, 1916, Vol. LXXXIV, col. 1683, 26 July 1916.

3   Ibid.

4   Ibid.

5   Ibid.

6   Thomas Burke, *City of Encounters: A London Divertissement* (London: Little, Brown, 1932).

7   *The Times,* 15 November 1915.

8   28 December 1915, The Lilly Library, Mss department, Indiana University, Bloomington, Indiana, Thomas Burke Papers.

9   Caradoc Evans, 'A Bundle of Memories', *The Book of Fleet Street*, T. Michael Pope, ed. (London: Cassell & Co., 1930), p. 94. Melrose published Caradoc Evans'

My People (1915). Stories about his native Wales that caused outrage for their portrayal of Welsh narrow mindedness and sexual repression.

10   Stanley Unwin, *The Truth About a Publisher: An Autobiographical Record* (London: George Allen and Unwin, 1960), p. 133.

11   John Harris, ed., *Fury Never Leaves Us: A Miscellany of Caradoc Evans* (Bridgend: Poetry Wales Press, 1985), p. 120.

12   Grant Richards, *Author Hunting by an Old Literary Sportsman* (London: Hamish Hamilton, 1934), pp. 236–7.

13   September 1916, The Lilly Library, Mss department, Indiana University, Bloomington, Indiana, Thomas Burke Papers.

14   *Times Literary Supplement*, 28 September 1916, p. 464.

15   *The Best Stories of Thomas Burke,* selected with a foreword by John Gawsworth (London: Phoenix House, 1950), pp. 8–9.

16   Arthur Winnington-Ingram, *Cleansing London: Addresses Delivered in Connections with the National Mission of Repentance and Hope* (London: C. Arthur Pearson Ltd., 1916), p. 25.

17   Letter from H. G. Wells to Burke, n.d., Burke Mss., The Lilly Library.

18   W. R. Colton cited in Samuel Hynes, *A War Imagined:*

The First World War and English Culture (London: Pimlico, 1990), p. 58.

19   Ibid., p. 12.

20   Sax Rohmer, *The Mystery of Dr Fu-Manchu* (London: Methuen, 1913).

21   Thomas Burke, *English Night-Life: From Norman Curfew to Present Black-Out* (B. T. Batsford Ltd., 1941), p. 114.

22   James Greenwood, *Low-Life Deeps: An Account of the Strange Fish to be Found There* (London: Chatto & Windus, 1876), pp. 118–9. See also Greenwood's, 'An opium smoke in Tiger Bay', in *In Strange Company: Being the Experiences of a Roving Correspondent* (London: Vizitelly & Co., 1883).

23   Charles Dickens, *The Mystery of Edwin Drood* (London: The Classics Book Club, 1942 (1870)), p. 2.

24   Oscar Wilde, *The Picture of Dorian Gray* (Ware, Hertfordshire: Wordsworth Editions Ltd., 1992 (1890)), p. 148.

25   Cited in Virginia Berridge, *Opium and the People: Opiate Use and Drug Control Policy in Nineteenth and Early-Twentieth Century England* (London & New York: Free Association Books, 1999), p. 198.

26   James Platt, 'Chinese London and Its Opium Dens', *The Gentleman's Magazine,* 279 (1895), p. 273.

27   Walter Besant, *East London* (London: Chatto & Windus, 1901), pp. 205–206.

28 George A. Wade, 'The Cockney John Chinaman', *The English Illustrated Magazine* (July 1900), pp. 301–307.

29 Count E. Armfelt, 'Oriental London', collected in *Living London,* vol.1, ed. by George Sims (London: Cassell & Co. Ltd., 1902–3), pp. 81–87.

30 *Leslie's Illustrated Newspaper,* 18 December 1875.

31 Sir Charles Wentworth Dilke, *A Record of Travel in English Speaking Countries* (1885), pp.186–7, cited in William Purviance Fenn, 'Ah Sin And His Brethren in American Literature', *Publications of the College of Chinese Studies,* 7 (1933), p. 16.

32 Michael Keevak, *Becoming Yellow: A Short History of Racial Thinking* (New Jersey: Princeton University Press, 2011), p 124.

33 Charles H. Pearson, *National Life and Character, A Forecast* (London: Macmillan, 1893).

34 The 'trouble' was the Kiaochow incident which led to the Scramble for Concessions in Qing China. It was published in twenty parts (5 February – 18 June). Grant Richards wrote for W. T. Stead's *Review of Reviews* (1890–96) before setting up his own firm.

35 M. P. Shiel, *The Yellow Danger* (1898), p 18.

36 W. T. Stead, *Review of Reviews* (Feb 1895).

37 W. T. Stead, *Review of Reviews* (March 1895).

38 Ibid.

39   Ibid., p 273.

40   *The New York Times*, 16 July 1900.

41   *The Times*, 17 July 1900, p 9.

42   *Manchester Evening Chronicle,* 1905.

43   *Daily Mail* (December 1906).

44   Gregory B. Lee, *Troubadours, Trumpeters, Troubled Makers: Lyricism, Nationalism and Hybridity in China and Its Others* (London: Hurst and Company 1996), p. 206.

45   'Chinatown in Liverpool: Indignant Protest', *Daily Mail* (December 1906).

46   Rohmer, *The Yellow Claw* (London: Methuen, 1915).

47   Cay Van Ash and Elizabeth Rohmer, *Master of Villainy: A Biography of Sax Rohmer* (Ohio: Bowling Green University Popular Press, 1972), p. 77

48   Measuring Worth <http://www.measuringworth.com/index.php> accessed 2 September 2014.

49   Edward Tupper, *Seamen's Torch: The Life Story of Captain Edward Tupper, National Union of Seamen* (London: Hutchinson & Co 1938), cited in Ross Forman, *China and the Victorian Imagination: Empires Entwined* (Cambridge: Cambridge University Press, 2013), p.165.

50   White, *Zeppelin Nights*, p. 195.

51   Rohmer, *The Yellow Claw*.

52   Ibid., pp. 421–2.

53   W. Locke, *Stories of the Land we Live in* (1878), p. 9.

54 Joseph Conrad, *Heart of Darkness* (London: Sovereign Press, 2012 (1899), p. 9.

55 Rohmer, *Yellow Shadows* (London: Cassell, 1925).

56 Burke, *The Wind and the Rain: A Book of Confessions* (London: Thornton Butterworth Ltd., 1924), p. 136.

57 Burke, *Out and About: A Notebook of London in Wartime* (London: George Allen and Unwin, 1919), p. 33.

58 Burke, *Nights in Town*, (London: George Allen and Unwin, 1916), p. 91.

59 Burke, *Out and About*, pp. 39–41.

60 Marek Kohn, *Dope Girls: The Birth of the British Drug Underground* (London: Granta Publications 2001), p. 30.

61 *The Athenaeum*, 16 May 1919, p. 336.

62 Burke, *Out and About*, p. 43.

63 Letter to Isabel Pound, 15 March 1909, cited in Rebecca Beasley *Ezra Pound and the Visual Culture of Modernism* (Cambridge: Cambridge University Press, 2007), p. 60.

64 Brigit Patmore, *My Friends When Young* (London: Heinemann, 1968), p. 75.

65 Omar Pound and A. Walton Litz eds., *Ezra Pound and Dorothy Shakespear: Their Letters 1909-1914* (New York: New Directions, 1984), p. 267.

66 *Fortnightly Review*, 1 September 1914.

67 3 September 1916. Cited in Zhaoming Qian, *The Modernist Response to Chinese Art: Pound, Moore,*

Stevens (Virginia: University of Virginia Press, 2003), p.18.

68 Cited in Hynes, *A War Imagined*.

69 Burke, *Living in Bloomsbury* (London: George Allen and Unwin, 1947 (1939)), p. 44.

70 Burke, *London In My Time* (London: Rich & Cowan Ltd., 1934).

71 Pound and Litz eds., *Ezra Pound and Dorothy Shakespear: Their Letters 1909-1914* (New York: New Directions, 1984), p. 264. The notorious Brilliant Chang had a share in a Chinese restaurant in Regent Street as reported in the *Daily Express* (11 April 1924). Various members of its staff were arrested for supplying cocaine.

72 Burke, *Out and About*, p. 52.

73 Claire Tomalin, *Katherine Mansfield: A Secret Life* (London: Viking, 1987), p. 60.

74 Ford Madox Ford, *The Marsden Case* (London: Duckworth & Co., 1923), p. 43.

75 Ibid., p.76.

76 *The Connoisseur*, vol. 40 (May 1915), p. 56.

77 Jacob Epstein, *Let There Be Sculpture* (New York: G. B. Putnam & Sons, 1940), p. 100.

78 Augustus John's description, see Michael Holroyd, *Augustus John* (London: Chatto & Windus, 1996), p. 418.

79 Rohmer, *The Yellow Claw*.

80   De Rachewiltz, M., Moody, A. and Moody, J., *Ezra Pound to His Parents: Letters 1895-1929* (Oxford: Oxford University Press, 2011), p. 334.

81   Hugh Kenner, *The Pound Era* (Berkeley: University of California Press, 1971), p. 202.

82   Ibid.

83   4 Oct 1891– 5 June 1915. His was death announced in the second issue of *BLAST.*

84   Introduction to *Selected Poems,* edited and with an introduction by T. S. Eliot (London: Faber & Gwyer, 1928).

85   A. David Moody, *Ezra Pound: Poet. Vol. 1: The Young Genius 1885-1920* (Oxford: Oxford University Press, 2009), p. 267.

86   Ford Madox Ford, *Thus to Revisit* (London: E. P. Dutton & Co., 1921), p. 180.

87   Ibid.

88   *The Globe*, 29 December 1917.

89   *The Pall Mall Gazette,* 29 December 1917.

90   *The Morning Post*, 27 December, 1917.

91   *The Stage*, 27 December 1917.

92   *Chu Chin Chow* became the longest running show on stage with 2235 performances at Her Majesty's Theatre in London, opening on 31 August 1916. See Brian Singleton, *Oscar Asche, Orientalism, And British Musical Comedy* (Praeger: Connecticut and London, 2004).

93   Clive Barker, 'Theatre and society: the Edwardian legacy,' in Clive Barker and Maggie B. Gale, eds., *British Theatre between the Wars 1918-1939* (Cambridge: Cambridge University Press, 2000), p. 13.

94   Robert Bickers, *Britain In China: Community, Culture and Colonialism 1900-1949* (Manchester: Manchester University Press, 1999), p. 49.

95   Review of *San Toy* in *The Illustrated Sporting And Dramatic News*, 329, 4 November 1899.

96   Cited in Gordon Williams, *British Theatre in the Great War: A Revaluation*, (London and New York: Continuum, 2005), p.18.

97   *Daily Mirror*, 4 September 1917.

98   *Morning Post*, 13 June 1924.

99   D. H. Lawrence, 'Matriarchy' in *Evening News*, 5 October 1928.

100 Theatre Critic, Huntly Carter, cited in Barker, 'Theatre and Society', p. 11.

101 Lawrence, 'Matriarchy', *Evening News*.

102 Singleton, *Oscar Asche*, p. 109.

103 Ibid., p. 133.

104 F. Vernon, *The Twentieth Century Theatre* (London: Harrap & Co. Ltd., 1924), pp. 220–1.

105 *The Tatler*, 293, 6 September 1916.

106 St John Ervine, *The Organised Theatre: A Plea in Civics* (London: George Allen and Unwin, 1924), p. 7.

107 Burke, *Out and About*, pp. 66–7.

108 Robert Bickers, 'New Light on Lao She, London and the London Missionary Society, 1921-1929', *Modern Chinese Literature*, 8 (1994), p. 33.

109 *China Express and Telegraph,* 31 May 1928.

110 Thomas Burke, *London In My Time* (London: Rich & Cowan Ltd., 1934; New York: Loring & Mussey, 1935), p. 126.

111 Burke, *London In My Time*, p. 126, also see Berridge on the wartime cocaine epidemic, *Opium And The People*, p. 249. Also see Kohn, *Dope Girls*, Chapter 2, 'Snow On Their Boots'.

112 Diana Cooper, *An Autobiography* (London: M. Russell, 1979), p. 97.

113 See Kohn, *Dope Girls*, p. 31.

114 Ibid.

115 Lynn Pan, *Sons of the Yellow Emperor: The Story of Overseas Chinese* (London: Secker & Warburg, 1990), p. 87.

116 *The Sketch*, 27 November 1918.

117 *Devon and Exeter Gazette*, 9 September 1916.

118 Ibid.

119 Ibid.

120 *Liverpool Post and Mercury*, 15 September 1916.

121 See Paul Greenhalgh, *Ephemeral Vistas: The Expositions Universelles, Great Exhibitions and Worlds Fairs, 1851 - 1939* (Manchester: Manchester University Press, 1988), pp. 96–9. He cites from

Frank Leslie's *Illustrated Historical Register of the Centennial Exposition 1876* (Philadelphia, 1876), facsimile available (New York: Paddington Press, 1984). See also *Ephemeral Vistas,* p. 110, fn. 5.

122 Waller, 'Immigration into Britain: The Chinese', pp. 12–13.

123 Rohmer, *The Yellow Claw*, p. 59.

124 *The Syracuse Herald*, 15 June 1919.

125 Kohn, *Dope Girls*, p. 85.

126 Rohmer, *Dope: A Story of Chinatown and the Drug Traffic* (London: Cassell, 1919).

127 Rohmer, *The Yellow Claw*, p. 123.

128 Rohmer, *Dope*, p. 115. For further discussion of the cultural mythmaking of Chinese Limehouse see Witchard, Thomas Burke's *Dark Chinoiserie: Limehouse Nights* and the *Queer Spell of Chinatown* (Farnham: Ashgate, 2009).

129 Ibid.

130 Kohn, *Dope Girls*, p. 162.

131 Ibid.

132 *World's Pictorial News*, April 1924.

133 *Evening News,* 25, 27 April 1922.

134 *Evening News,* 24 Feb 1922.

135 The Godfrey Edition, Old Ordnance Survey Maps, 'Stepney and Limehouse 1914', (repr. 1999).

136 *The Sphere*, 164, 8 May 1926.

137 *The Journal of Arnold Bennett* (London: The Viking

Press, 1933), p. 823.

138 Burke gives this date for the story in a letter to Earle J. Bernheimer, n.d., Burke Mss., Lilly Library.

139 'Chong Ching, Chong Sam, Wong Ho, Yow Yip, Choi Sau, Ah Chong Koon, Pong Peng, Cheng Pong Lai, are a few names taken at random from a collection of application forms for ration books during the First World War'. See 'Our Fascinating Borough', *Tower Hamlets News,* vol 1., no. 4., p. 3, Chinatown File, Local History Archive, Tower Hamlets Central Library.

140 *The Sphere,* 164, 8 May 1926.

141 Bickers, *Britain in China,* p. 52.

142 *Daily Mirror,* 21 November 1934.

143 *Evening News,* 11 April 1931.

144 Instead remarking briefly: 'Until recent years it was known as the Chinese Quarter, in an unpleasant sense: a locality of shady opium dens and resorts of rowdy inebriety.' *London: A Combined Guidebook & Atlas* (London: Thos. Cook & Son Ltd., 1937), p. 47.

145 'Limehouse "Debunked"', unattributed newspaper clipping (1934), Chinatown File, Local History Archive, Tower Hamlets Central Library.

The Penguin China Specials: First World War Series

The First World War may well have been the twentieth century's most significant event, its myriad ripple effects and consequences are still being felt today. However, to date, it has mostly been seen from a European perspective, images of brave, young soldiers in the trenches have, quite rightly, been seared deep on the collective consciousness of the West and their sacrifice should never be forgotten. That said, as with most things in life, the war was far more complex than that and it led – both directly and indirectly – to the Bolshevik Revolution in Russia, the May Fourth Movement in China and Japanese imperialism in the Far East, as well as, of course, the Second World War and its resulting Cold War. To mark its centenary Penguin is publishing a series of Specials which will look at the conflict from a different perspective.

If you enjoyed this Penguin China Special why not try another in the First World War series:

The Siege of Tsingtao: The only battle of the First World War to be fought in Asia by Jonathan Fenby

The Chinese Labour Corps: The Forgotten Chinese Labourers of the First World War by Mark O'Neill

Betrayal in Paris: How the Treaty of Versailles Led to China's Long Revolution by Paul French

Getting Stuck in for Shanghai by Robert Bickers

From the Tsar's Railway to the Red Army: The Experience of Chinese Labourers in Russia During the First World War and Bolshevik Revolution by Mark O'Neill

Picnics Prohibited: China in the First World War by Frances Wood

England's Yellow Peril: Sinophobia and the Great War by Anne Witchard